GREAT MARKETING

BULLET GUIDE

Fabienne Reynolds

Hodder Education, 338 Euston Road, London NW1 3BH

Hodder Education is an Hachette UK company

First published in UK 2011 by Hodder Education

This edition published 2011

Copyright © 2011 Fabienne Reynolds

The moral rights of the author have been asserted

Database right Hodder Education (makers)

Artworks (internal and cover): Peter Lubach

Cover concept design: Two Associates

British Library Cataloguing in Publication Data: a catalogue record for this title is available from the British Library.

10 9 8 7 6 5 4 3 2 1

The publisher has used its best endeavours to ensure that any website addresses referred to in this book are correct and active at the time of going to press. However, the publisher and the author have no responsibility for the websites and can make no guarantee that a site will remain live or that the content will remain relevant, decent or appropriate.

The publisher has made every effort to mark as such all words which it believes to be trademarks. The publisher should also like to make it clear that the presence of a word in the book, whether marked or unmarked, in no way affects its legal status as a trademark.

Every reasonable effort has been made by the publisher to trace the copyright holders of material in this book. Any errors or omissions should be notified in writing to the publisher, who will endeavour to rectify the situation for any reprints and future editions.

Hachette UK's policy is to use papers that are natural, renewable and recyclable products and made from wood grown in sustainable forests. The logging and manufacturing processes are expected to conform to the environmental regulations of the country of origin.

www.hoddereducation.co.uk

Typeset by Stephen Rowling/Springworks

Printed in Spain

'Success depends upon previous preparation, and without such preparation there is sure to be failure.'

Confucius

About the author

Fabienne Reynolds has been a marketing and PR professional for more than 20 years and runs her own consultancy. She specializes in marketing strategies, product launch plans, copywriting and business development.

She holds the Chartered Institute of Marketing Diploma and the Professional Freelance Journalism Diploma.

Acknowledgements

Everyone at Hodder Education – especially my publishers Victoria Roddam and Sam Richardson, and Alison Frecknall who 'discovered' me – has been a pleasure to work with. Special thanks to Professor Malcolm McDonald, who has been an inspiration throughout my marketing career and kindly contributed an overview on the importance of a marketing strategy. Thanks also to the Peter Drucker Society for giving me permission to use one of his citations.

Fabienne Reynolds, Steyning, West Sussex
June 2011

Contents

Introduction

Understanding the basics of marketing is the first step any business should take

There are an estimated 4.8 million private sector enterprises in the UK, accounting for 99% of all businesses. Almost all of these are small and employ up to nine employees.* With constraints on budgets and resources, marketing is often out of their reach. While it is clear that **the purpose of marketing is to add value**, it is very rare to come across a dedicated marketing function in a small business. Such activities are often handled randomly with varying degrees of success.

Understanding the basics of marketing is the first step any business should take. Equipped with this knowledge, companies can assess **what will work for them** and, in the process, **save time and money**.

This book is designed to serve as an introduction to marketing and **presents the essentials in an easy-to-digest format**. It outlines the marketing process using a step-by-step approach to help readers achieve a sense of what is required to add value to a business.

The purpose of this book is to provide **an insight into marketing and an overview of its fundamental aspects to anyone interested in the subject**. It will be of particular interest to small business owners and sole traders, anyone thinking of launching a start-up and those who would like to understand more about marketing without having to spend a considerable amount of time reading and learning about it.

For anyone wishing to explore the subject further, a list of recommended titles is given at the end of the book.

*Source: *Small and Medium Enterprise Statistics for the UK and Regions*, Department for Business, Innovation and Skills

1 What is marketing?

It's simpler than you think

Concepts such as SWOT (strengths, weaknesses, opportunities and threats) analysis, brand awareness and customer relationship management may seem complicated at first but these activities can have an impact on **revenue** and help achieve **customer retention**.

Fast-changing technology means that marketing is always evolving – today, for example, activities such as **online marketing** and **social networking** are becoming increasingly important. It is impossible to be an expert in all areas but by focusing on the right communications, businesses can **create value** and **enhance their product or service**.

To make a profit you have to have the right product in front of the right people

Marketing is not a complicated subject but there is still confusion about what it is or isn't. Successful marketing relies on a combination of a **long-term strategy** and **short-term action plans**.

To achieve this, one must **research, evaluate and establish** the goals (or objectives) and determine which activities (or tactics) can be used to achieve them. **Knowing your market and customers** is the first step in the process.

Definitions of marketing

The Chartered Institute of Marketing currently defines marketing as:

'The management process responsible for identifying, anticipating and satisfying customer requirements profitably.'

Another definition is:

'The aim of marketing is to know and understand the customer so well the product or service fits him and sells itself.'

Peter F. Drucker, *Management: Tasks, Responsibilities, Practices*

In brief, marketing is:

* **maximizing** sales opportunities and growing the business by **engaging** with customers who need or want what you have to offer *and*
* using the right **communication channels** to reach them and **constantly adapting** to their needs so they keep coming back.

An early effort at direct marketing

In ancient Rome, ladies engaged in the world's oldest profession allegedly wore sandals which left imprints of the words 'follow me' on the city's dusty roads.

Marketing at a glance

The biggest problem all businesses have – big and small – is developing a winning strategy. It is rarely the quality of the product or service that is the cause of failure. Rather, it is a failure to understand the market, how the market works, what the key segments are, what the real needs are of the customers in these segments and, above all, why they should buy your product rather than that of your competitors. Once you have done this, it is crucial to know how you intend to communicate your offer to your key target markets. No matter what anyone says, this is the core secret of successful strategies.

Professor Malcolm McDonald

Marketing is a continuous process that involves researching, planning, promoting and evaluating results:

* **research** – your market, customers and prospects
* **assess** – market opportunities
* **develop** – your marketing strategy
* **plan** – your key messages and activities
* **promote** – your products or services and your business
* **evaluate** – your successes and failures
* **adapt** – to meet customers' expectations.

Even the best product won't sell if no one wants it

Explaining the process

Marketing is not:

* a science
* an art
* a game
* just selling
* just advertising
* a one-way communication.

8

Now consider this example:

Actions	Tactics
A farmer puts a sign in his field saying 'Farm shop, first left'	Advertising
He places a sign on his tractor with the location of his farm shop	Promotion
He drives it around during the town's festival and takes children on a brief tour	Publicity
A journalist from the local paper takes a photo and writes a short article	Public relations
Locals and visitors go to the farm shop, are shown around, hear how the products are made and purchase some of them	Sales
The farmer planned it all	Marketing

Keeping it simple

Before you can decide what you should
do, you need to know where you stand:

* **define** your market geographically and
  in terms of your products or services
* **establish** who your competitors
  are and where their strengths and
  weaknesses lie
* **talk** to your customers and assess
  their views of your company and
  products or services
* **evaluate** how this compares with
  what your competitors offer

* **think** about what you need to do to market your business to the right customers
* **establish** what is unique about your business and from this define your goals and messages
* **identify** where and how you should deliver these messages.

This should help you plan your marketing activities.

To fail to plan is to plan to fail

'Knowledge is of no value unless you put it into practice.'

Anton Chekhov

2 Marketing basics – the strategy

Strategies and plans

'Strategy: a plan of action designed to achieve a long-term or overall aim.'

Oxford Dictionary of English

Marketing is about letting people know about your products or services and persuading them to buy them. To achieve this, you will need both a **marketing strategy** and a **marketing plan**.

Some marketing strategies aim to capture a certain segment of the market, but for many small businesses, strategies tend to be much more generic in nature. But, where there is no strategy, there is often chaos.

Many small businesses confuse marketing strategy with marketing plans:

* a marketing strategy is derived from the business plan and determines the approach for achieving the business objectives
* the marketing strategy summarizes how to position a company's products while the marketing plan contains the specific activities required in order to achieve the marketing objectives.

A marketing strategy document should therefore include:

* an overview of the business and its objectives
* an overview of its products or services
* a profile of its customers
* a competitors' analysis *and*
* the marketing goals.

Developing a marketing strategy

The development of a marketing strategy is a process made up of several stages:

Business Plan	Company Mission Statement – values, vision and purpose of the business
	↓
	Corporate Objectives – business goals (profit, growth, etc.)
	↓
	Corporate Strategy – direction the business should take (e.g. market penetration)
Marketing Strategy	Marketing Objectives – the means by which to meet the business objectives
	↓
	Marketing Strategies – market and product strategies
	↓
Marketing Plan	Marketing Plan and Tactics – the actions to achieve the marketing objectives

Figure 2.1: The elements of a marketing strategy

CASE STUDY: A local greengrocer

Mission statement: to source and sell high-quality, locally grown fresh produce using sustainable farming practices.

Business objectives: to achieve sales of £500,000 in one year.

Corporate strategy: by increasing existing product range (product development).

The marketing objectives could be:

* to increase product awareness among existing customers by 30% in one year
* to inform target audiences about products, leading to a 10% increase in sales in one year
* to attract new customers from local catering businesses resulting in additional sales of 10% in the next 12 months.

Defining the marketing strategy

'Planning without action is futile, action without planning is fatal.'

Unknown author

The marketing strategy states the objectives and describes the way you are going to satisfy customers in your chosen markets.

If you do not know where you want to go, how can you possibly get there?

The marketing strategy will answer the 'how' question, while the marketing plan will explore the 'what, where and when'.

To determine your marketing strategy you must do the following:

* **review** the business objectives – is it to increase profits and, if so, by how much?
* **describe** your products – what is unique about them?
* **define** your desired audience – who they are, where they are
* **study** the competition – who they are and what they do
* **list** your strengths and weaknesses
* **identify** opportunities and threats.

If you do not know where you want to go, how can you possibly get there?

If you do not know where you want to go, how can you possibly get there?

Business strategies

There are only a few directions in which a business can go but there may be more than one strategy it can follow, such as market penetration and product development:

	Existing markets	New markets
Existing products	Market penetration (sell more to existing customers)	Market development (identify new customers for existing products)
New products	Product development (sell new products to existing customers)	Diversification (offer new products to new customers)

Adapted from Ansoff Matrix

In the example of the greengrocer given earlier in this chapter, the strategy combines product development and market development.

20

Developing the marketing objectives

To start with, the marketing objectives can be broadly defined. Once you have formulated the marketing strategy, these will need to be reviewed and adjusted.

The marketing objectives should be feeding directly from the business plan. In other words, if market penetration is desired, marketing should consider how it can help increase sales of existing products to current customers, given the market conditions and the competitive landscape.

If a company has, say, a 20% market share, new sales will need to be generated from existing customers and the first role of marketing will be first to identify the potential for such an increase.

'Before beginning, plan carefully.'
Marcus Tullius Cicero

The marketing strategy process

You have already incorporated your mission statement, business strategy and objectives and this gives you some sense of direction, but you need to incorporate other elements before you can start mapping out your marketing strategy. These are:

* SWOT analysis
* competitor analysis
* customer profile
* opportunities and threats.

These need not be daunting, and for a small business should be fairly easy to conduct. They will, however, prove invaluable in your understanding of where your business stands and what its chances of success might be. You will also be able to spot any gaps in the market.

CASE STUDY: Selling fresh milk

Let's evaluate the opportunity for selling fresh milk in a greengrocer's shop. Without a formal plan and understanding of market conditions, demand for the product and competitors, it may be a completely wasted initiative.

Knowing where customers currently buy their milk, what type and at what price is invaluable. If the greengrocer were the only shop within a two-mile radius, this would be an excellent opportunity to provide residents with a convenience that is currently unavailable.

Should there, however, be a mini-supermarket within the vicinity, the outlet would need to consider either a niche market, such as fresh organic milk, or a price promotion so that it is competitive.

3 Knowledge is power

Know your market and customers

The owner of any business should continually assess its potential for success and ask the following questions:

* is there demand for my products or services?
* what price are customers prepared to pay for them?
* who are my customers today and how can I communicate with them?
* what could I do differently to ensure they remain loyal to me?

With this information in hand, businesses can start drafting their marketing strategy.

Marketing could be the differentiator between success and failure

Coca-Cola

In 1985, following some blind tests by the company and in an effort to counteract the increasing popularity of Pepsi, Coca-Cola changed the original formula of its famous drink. The new product was a total flop as the company had failed to evaluate the consumer loyalty to the product prior to replacing the formula.

Every business is unique and requires a marketing strategy based on:

* its size
* the economic conditions
* its competitors
* the demographics and profile of its customers *and*
* the area in which it operates.

SWOT analysis

'You can't expect to meet the challenges of today with yesterday's tools and expect to be in business tomorrow.'

Unknown author

The internal factors

* Strengths should include unique features of your products or services, such as excellent customer service or the commitment of the sales team.
* Weaknesses may comprise the limitation of resources, such as staff, the length of time the business has been established or the fact that you do not have a website.

The external factors

* Your opportunities could be the lack of competition in your local area or your specialization in a particular field.
* Threats may include the limited financial resources of your existing customers or the length of time your competitors have been established.

28

What to consider when conducting a SWOT analysis:

	Strengths	Weaknesses
Internal factors	Location Experience Product/Service Distribution/Price Quality Resources/Assets Customer relationship Management Financials Marketing experience	Location Experience Product/Service Distribution/Price Quality Resources/Assets Customer relationship Management Financials Marketing experience
	Opportunities	Threats
External factors	Customer needs Markets Economics Technology Politics Taxes Distribution channels	Customer needs Markets Economics Technology Politics Taxes Distribution channels

Seeing the big picture

The SWOT analysis is useful to establish the overall strategic position of a business. When doing the exercise, be realistic and objective.

✳ To avoid bias, ask key members of staff to conduct their own SWOT analysis independently. You can then compare findings and get a pretty good idea of where your business currently stands.

✳ Ideas may also arise from the exercise, such as the opportunity to develop a new distribution channel and potentially increase demand for your products.

If our greengrocer were to evaluate the potential of adding free delivery to his service, he would be in a better position to compete.

The SWOT analysis is useful to establish the overall strategic position of a business

Don't forget to:

* look at the opportunities in relation to your strengths
* evaluate the threats in view of your weaknesses
* establish your potential in view of your core competences
* measure the risk in view of your capabilities.

CASE STUDY: Seizing opportunities

Having relocated to larger premises, our greengrocer found a new opportunity: selling locally brewed beer in reusable containers of various sizes to accommodate the needs of different customers, from couples to students.

Targeting the right customers

You cannot sell indiscriminately to everyone. You need to assess who is most likely to need your products or services.

Questions you should ask include:

* what are the needs of my customers?
* which customers will get me the most profits?
* how can I reach them?
* how can I improve my customer service and increase profits?
* what changes can I introduce to increase customer retention?
* what would be the most effective pricing strategy?
* what are the best means of distributing and selling my products or services?

The answers to these questions will help you draw an accurate profile of your ideal customers.

Some useful tips

✔ Try to assess how customer behaviour has changed since you have been in business (such as purchasing patterns)

✔ Are there any trends under way that you can anticipate?

✔ Is the economic climate likely to affect what customers buy and the way they buy it?

✔ Will they have need for your products or services if budgets are cut or there is a sudden boom?

✔ List the main benefits that your customers will receive by doing business with you

✔ Keep adding something new to generate more sales

✔ Aim at becoming a valuable resource to your customers

✔ Anticipate changes in your market – your marketing strategy should be flexible enough to accommodate them

✔ Set up email alerts to keep an eye on your competitors

Analysis

A good marketing strategy is based on an analysis of the different needs of your customers, your strengths and weaknesses, and upcoming opportunities and threats.

Start thinking about what you need to do to market your business to the right people:

* are there perhaps customers you don't currently target?
* could you sell more to your existing customers?
* is there a service you could add?
* is your complaints process satisfactory?
* have you lost any customers to a competitor?

The more information you gather, the better equipped you will be to target the right people for the right reasons.

If 20% of your customers generate 80% of your revenue, you need to assess two things:

1 why 80% of customers spend less
2 how you can reach more customers like the existing 20%.

The majority of your customers may need less of what you have to offer but perhaps it is not clear to them what else you provide. It is easier and less expensive to retain customers than to seek new ones.

If you only sell to a small proportion of your target market, you need to know where the rest buys from and why. Knowing how your prices, products and after-sales service compare with competitors will be key in helping you to position your products and services effectively.

The more information you gather, the better equipped you will be to target the right people

4 Why research matters

Knowing your competitors

In an ideal world, every company would have unique products for the unique needs of its customers. In this world, there would be no competitors:

* you could charge customers whatever you liked
* you would not need a sales team
* you could spend little or no money on promotion
* customer service would seem superfluous.

But would your customers be satisfied?

How long would it be until someone looked at your business model and found a way to offer the same but better or cheaper? And once they did, what would happen to your business? The likelihood is that it would fail – unless you were able to adapt.

Competition is healthy and ensures that customers get a choice and a fair deal

Competition is healthy and ensures that customers get a choice and a fair deal. They are able to compare products and services and choose those that best match their needs, budgets and expectations.

But competition can provide a fierce environment in which to operate. A local shop may find itself in a very tight position when a supermarket opens a new branch. Its only choices may be to close down or find a way to diversify, but doing nothing is not an option.

Analysing your competitors

'If you know the enemy and know yourself, you need not fear the result of a hundred battles. If you know yourself but not the enemy, for every victory gained you will also suffer a defeat.'

Sun Tzu, *The Art of War*

Your competitors are the companies with whom you compete for market share. They offer similar products to the same customers. Their objective is also to grow and succeed.

A **competitors' analysis** enables a company to understand its position in the market. There are three stages involved in such an analysis:

1 finding information
2 analysing it
3 using it in your business strategy.

Why do a competitors' analysis?:

* to know who they are and what they do
* to understand how they do it
* to assess if they do it better or worse
* to know their weaknesses and strengths
* to create opportunities for yourself.

Unless your products or services are unique or better priced or have features over and above those of your competitors, selling a product or service that has no more to offer than anyone else's places you in the 'me too' category. Why would anyone buy anything from you if there was no distinct advantage in doing so?

A competitors' analysis helps businesses to establish where they stand and identify their competitive advantage. It may also highlight new opportunities for your business.

Gathering competitor information

Here are some sources from where you can gather information about your competitors:

* your customers
* your suppliers
* your sales teams
* purchasing departments
* trade publications and the media
* market research
* the Internet (websites, forums and social media)
* trade shows and conferences
* publicly available data.

Competitive information (or intelligence) provides a business with the facts on which to base its marketing, product launches and overall business strategy. Not all information may be relevant or useful and the next stage involves sifting through the data to identify the important facts.

The analysis

What you should know	What would be nice to know
Product features	Research and development plans
Sales	Costs
Profits	Customer satisfaction
Pricing	Product strategies
Market share	Marketing effectiveness
Structure	Future plans
Marketing strategy	Suppliers' contractual terms
Suppliers	Customer database quality
Management structure	Impending business issues
Strategic partnerships	

A competitors' analysis will help management understand their competitive position and should include existing as well as potential competitors.

Ways to beat the competition
When communicating with customers, explain how you are different from your competitors

Exploit their weaknesses

* Whatever weaknesses you have identified in your competitors' products or services, marketing or distribution, these could present opportunities for your business.
* Depending on the market in which you operate, it could be poor customer service or ordering facilities. In a competitive market, you could turn this to your advantage. Exploit any weakness and assess if this is something you could offer.
* Even if your position is good, don't be complacent as your strengths may change and your competitors could adopt and improve on them. Anticipate and plan your own improvements.

Undermine their strengths

* Evaluate the information you find about your competitors. It may help you to spot gaps in the market and highlight less competitive areas for you to explore.
* If they do something better than you, introduce something yourself. You could improve on your products, services or your customer service. You could review your prices, change your promotional materials or offer online ordering.
* Try to identify if there are things you could do better to add value. When communicating with customers, explain how you are different from your competitors.

● 'I see a gap in the market.'

Identifying your competitive advantage

Once you have analysed the competition and understood your place in the market, you should be able to establish how you can better position your business.

Create a chart with your key findings:

	Our business	Competitor A	Competitor B	Competitor C
Products	Product X and Y	Product X	Product Y	Product X and Y
Price	Average	Low	Average	High
Strengths	Good customer service Product Y recently improved	Strong sales team Low production costs	Good after-sales service Established network of business partners	Outstanding customer relations Established 15 years Online ordering Strong marketing focus
Weaknesses	No online ordering No proactive marketing	Poor customer service Product X low quality	No website Product slightly dated No proactive selling	Expensive products Focus on high end of market

Now add your opportunities and threats:

	Our business	Competitor A	Competitor B	Competitor C
Opportunities	Develop website to offer online ordering Develop marketing initiatives	Improve customer service	Create website Upgrade product Recruit sales team	Launch product Z that combines benefits of X and Y Reduce rates to attract new customers
Threats	Competitor C starting to target lower end of market	New company offering product at low prices	Slow economy forcing customers to reduce spend	Competitor B introducing product Z

As you map out your findings, you should start to see a clearer picture. In this example, competitor C presents the most risks, while competitor B could become a strong contender.

TOP TIP
Setting up social media alerts via Google is a good way of keeping an eye on 'conversations' taking place about your competitors. You'll be the first to hear the good and the bad!

5 Getting started – setting the objectives

Setting objectives

An objective describes a key focus area and expected results

· ·

With all the information in hand, it is time to **refine and adjust your marketing objectives**. These should take into consideration what you know about your business, customers and competitors.

To set a realistic and achievable objective you will need to define:

* the target market
* the potential for that market
* the success rate you can expect
* the date by which it can be achieved.

Bullet Guide: Great Marketing

An objective describes a key focus area and expected results. An advertising exercise may be one of the means used to promote products and services but this is a tactic, not an objective.

Very rarely would a marketing strategy have just one objective. If your research highlighted that some of your customers were not aware of your full product range, or that an existing product could be of interest to new customers, both should be considered.

Ultimately, all marketing objectives **focus on products and markets**. They work together to bring about increased awareness, sales and profit for the business by targeting the right markets at the right time, with the right products and for the right reasons.

SMART objectives

An objective should always be SMART:

* **S**pecific
* **M**easurable
* **A**chievable
* **R**ealistic
* **T**ime dependent

A marketing objective should help generate new sales. If it doesn't, it probably isn't right.

Consider these two examples:

1 to promote our existing product range to new customers and generate 100 new sales by the end of the year
2 to raise awareness of product X to existing customers by 30% by 30 June resulting in a 5% increase in sales.

Note how each has a specific goal, with measures and dates. To determine whether an objective is realistic and achievable, you will need to evaluate **past performance**, the **current competitive landscape** and **market trends** as well as assess if you have the necessary **resources** in place.

From objectives to strategies

The marketing strategy outlines how to achieve your marketing objectives and should include information about what is known as the **Four P's**:

1 **Product** – your products or services
2 **Price** – what you charge for your products or services
3 **Promotion** – how you promote them in your selected markets
4 **Place** – how you can place them in front of your customers

With your broad marketing objectives in mind, you will need to develop strategies that enable you to build on your strengths, reduce your weaknesses, maximize your opportunities and overcome any threats.

Types of marketing objectives

The different types of marketing objectives include:

* **profitability** objectives – which target earnings
* **market share** objectives – which focus on how much of the market you aim to gain
* **promotional** objectives – which are about creating or increasing awareness of your products or services
* **growth** objectives – which aim at increasing the size of your business.

Consider creating your objectives around the Four P's:

* **Product** objectives – do you need to adjust your key messages about features and benefits?
* **Price** objectives – do you need to adjust your pricing?
* **Promotional** objectives – do you need to increase brand awareness?
* **Place** objectives – do you need to review where your products are available?

54

● Tortoise: 'I bet I can get there before you.' Hare: 'Off you go then!'

If your business objective is to increase sales by 5% in one year, the opportunity may be to target a new market. One marketing objective could therefore focus on creating awareness of your products within that market.

Services companies may also want to consider setting objectives around the additional Three P's: Process (e.g. orders or refunds policy); People; and Physical evidence (e.g. case studies and testimonials).

Developing objectives

Here are some examples of how to develop marketing objectives:

Business goals	Business objectives	Marketing objectives
Market penetration	Increase profits by 2% in one year	To help generate 2% sales in one year
Market development	To secure additional 1% market share by end of December	To increase product awareness by 20% among target audience
Product development	Introduce two new product lines over two years to achieve 5% profit increase	To successfully launch and create interest for new products resulting in 5% additional sales in two years
Diversification	Increase profits by 10% over two years	To introduce new pricing structure and promotions plan to help secure 10% market share in two years

56

**'Yes, I sell people things they don't need.
I can't, however, sell them something
they don't want. Even with advertising.
Even if I were of a mind to.'**

John O'Toole

The role of marketing is to propose objectives that will help increase sales or achieve a higher market share. By how much, from where and over what timeframe are the key things you need to determine.

Now ask yourself some relevant questions:

* how many new sales are required to achieve the profit increase?
* which markets can we target?
* what opportunities are we capable of exploiting?
* can we further develop features or services?
* how many new sales can we realistically achieve in one year?

Marketing in action

The marketing objectives look at improving market share, sales volume and awareness of products or services. The marketing plan is derived from them and sets out how to achieve them.

Using advertising and publicity to build awareness of a new product is a strategy to achieve sales and generate the 10% market share required by the business. What type of advertising, where and when and with what message are the means by which the specific objective can be achieved.

An advertisement in a local newspaper or magazine – to announce the opening of a new shop, for example – is one of the tactics that can be used to create awareness.

Did you know?

The first paid advertisement dates back to 1836. It was for a newspaper in France.

Having established your objectives, start thinking about what you need to do to reach the right people:

* research how you can reach them (online or offline)
* identify what you can promote to add value (such as free delivery)
* try to anticipate objections and ways to overcome them
* don't try to be all things to all customers – be specific!

TOP TIP
Even if your budgets are limited, there are many tactics that can be used to develop your marketing plan. An online British store selling British produce to expats can raise its profile by providing useful answers to forum questions.

6 The elements of marketing

From objectives to tactics

You need to determine the best way to achieve your marketing objectives. To do this, start by **outlining specific strategies** for each one.

If your marketing objective is to increase sales by 5%, one of your approaches could be to promote your products through local advertising. Another could be the use of social media to raise awareness of your website. Once you have formulated the specific strategies for achieving your objectives, the overall marketing strategy is finalized and you can start drafting the detailed marketing plan and tactics.

Marketing tactics are short-term actions designed to achieve the implementation of a strategy

Having identified the opportunities for your business and set the marketing objectives, the next stage involves investigating **the tools at your disposal** which will give you the best chances of success.

This section introduces the options available to meet different types of objectives and sets out **how to evaluate their potential effectiveness**. From advertising to word of mouth, each can be used and detailed in your marketing plan.

The aim is to gain an understanding of what you can do (given the size of your business), the potential results and the level of investment required (financial or other).

Strategies versus tactics

Tactics are the specific actions needed to support the marketing strategies and focus on their implementation.

The overall marketing strategy is **the process that analyses the current situation** (SWOT, customers, competitors) and defines the marketing objectives and proposed strategies (PR, advertising, etc.).

The marketing plan is the **detailed schedule of implementation** and includes activities, timescales, budgets, resources and ways to measure success.

Examples of **marketing strategies**:

* promote product through advertising
* set pricing to attract new customers
* PR campaign to announce new product.

Examples of **marketing tactics**:

✳ run monthly banner ad on website(s)
✳ offer online discount.

The marketing plan comprises a number of possible tactics that are the tools at your disposal to achieve the marketing objectives.

Once you have established the most suitable 'strategies' to reach your target customers, you will need to evaluate how much they cost and schedule their implementation. It is also important to devise ways of measuring their effectiveness, such as number of press cuttings for a PR campaign or number of online orders following an Internet marketing campaign.

Strategies around the Four P's

Promotion strategies

Promotion is about **communicating** the benefits of your products or services to your customers in order to **generate sales and profits**.

A communications programme, often referred to as the **promotional mix**, may consist of:

* advertising
* affiliate marketing
* direct mail
* email marketing
* personal selling
* point of sale
* networking

* exhibitions
* conferences
* public relations
* publicity
* sales promotion
* social media
* word of mouth.

'Creative without strategy is called "art". Creative with strategy is called "advertising".'

Jef I. Richards

Advertising is a popular promotional tool that has been used the world over as a way of communicating with existing and potential customers; it is perhaps the most difficult to evaluate. Advertising can take many forms (television, print, online, mobile) and costs will vary. A farmer can place a sign in one of his fields to promote his products at no cost but a campaign on local television may prove prohibitive.

A tale of two halves?

Lord Leverhulme (1851–1925), British founder of Unilever and philanthropist, said that half the money he spent on advertising was wasted – but he did not know which half.

Strategies around the Four P's (cont.)

Pricing strategies

Pricing strategies are derived from the business objectives:

* **penetration** – setting a low price to increase sales or market share
* **skimming** – the initial price is high then reduced to attract different types of customers
* **competition** – matching competitors' prices
* **product line** – offering different products in a range at different prices based on their specific features
* **bundle** – offering a group of products at a reduced price (lower than their cumulative value)
* **psychological** – matching market prices but rounded down such as £1.99 instead of £2
* **premium** – high price for exclusive products or services
* **optional** – optional extras are available at cost (popular with car manufacturers).

Place or distribution strategies

Place or distribution strategies refer to how a company makes its products or services available to customers. An efficient and effective distribution strategy is key to achieving the objectives.

Distribution can be direct, indirect or a combination of both:

* **indirect distribution** involves selling products or services through third parties – e.g. a farmer selling to a supermarket
* **direct distribution** involves distributing directly to the customer – e.g. the farmer having a farm shop.

● The Internet is an obvious distribution channel.

Strategies around the Four P's (cont.)
Product strategies

For small businesses, this is often about marketing the company rather than individual products. Product strategies comprise all the elements that together make up the product or service you offer. They can include:

* brand name
* features and functionality
* quality
* packaging
* instructions for use
* warranties
* customer service policies
* accessories.

A product or service needs to have the right features to appeal to the right customers. No amount of promotion is going to turn a bad product into a good one.

A product or service needs to have the right features to appeal to the right customers

People strategies

Adding a people strategy can add value to a customer experience, especially in the services industry.

Whether a customer purchases products or services in person, over the phone or via the Internet, customer-facing staff should be equipped with the information they need to deal efficiently with requests, queries or complaints.

Sales teams, customer service personnel and technical support staff should receive sufficient training to enable them to provide a good customer experience. Services companies also need to pay attention to their processes and the physical evidence they generate.

● 'The computer says NO!'

7 The marketing plan – defining the activities

Creating a marketing plan

The overall marketing strategy defines your target markets, marketing objectives, and positioning. Once the strategy is developed, you can start writing the marketing plan. The plan goes into much further detail and outlines how you are going to achieve the strategy. While a marketing strategy is a long-term document, marketing plans tend to be written every year.

Your marketing plan is your marketing strategy in action

The marketing plan is about how you intend to reach your objectives and deliver benefits to customers. It therefore includes action plans, budgets, timescales, resources and measurements.

By now you will have identified your target markets and positioning; you now need to consider and evaluate what tools are at your disposal to achieve each objective.

This chapter will guide you through the steps necessary to create **a marketing plan that works for you**.

Drawing up your plans

To help you write your own basic marketing strategy document, consider this example:

Business overview – what do you offer?	Circle of Friends – a reliable and trusted house-sitting service
Target market	Owners of exclusive homes in affluent areas who want peace of mind when on holidays
Competitors	Individuals offering house-sitting services; Large security firm in area
Competitive advantage – what sets you apart?	A small team of screened professionals introduced through personal recommendations; Cleaning during 'sitting' period; Pets taken care of
Business objectives	Increase number of 'sittings'; Increase profits
Marketing strategies – the top three things that are going to help	Personal selling; Direct mail; Advertising

And here's an example of a basic marketing plan for this business:

Tactics	Personal visits to Circle of Friends members for new introductions Direct mail to potential customers in targeted postcode areas Advertising in magazine(s) read by target customers Cocktail party for customers and guests
How much each programme will cost and contribute to my revenue (i.e. new sales expected)	Personal visits: £250 (conversion rate 20%) Direct mail: £100 (conversion rate 15%) Advertising: £1,000 (conversion rate 15%) Cocktail party: £1,000 (conversion rate 30%)
Timings	Personal visits: March Direct mail: April Advertising: April/May Cocktail party: May
Ownership	Personal visits and cocktail party: Sales director Advertising and direct mail: Marketing executive

From opportunity to tactics

> *I'm often asked what the secret is to creating a successful viral marketing campaign. It's really rather simple: give people something interesting or exciting to talk about and suggest simple ways they do this (online and off).*

Dan Hollings (www.danhollings.com)

Let's consider the business case for opening a lingerie shop in a small village…

Strengths:

* good supply of non-high street labels at a reasonable price.

Weaknesses:

* no previous experience as a retailer
* manager is also a member of staff.

Opportunities:

* no other lingerie shop nearby
* village is also a tourist destination
* previous lingerie shop had good turnover.

Threats:

* 60% of population are over 65
* local ladies boutique selling a small selection of quality undergarments
* target market is small.

Now let's set the objectives and tactics for this new business…

Marketing objectives:

* creating awareness among 20 to 55-year-old females within a 10-mile radius
* attracting customers to the store to achieve the required turnover (assuming 1 in 3 customers makes a purchase and the average sale is £30).

Strategies:

* promotion
* competitive pricing.

Tactics:

* publicity, advertising and word of mouth
* PR campaign and direct mail.

Promotion

Most small businesses focus their marketing strategies around promotion using the following techniques:

* Internet (website and directories)
* advertising (online and offline)
* direct marketing (by mail or email)
* public relations (to include publicity)
* events (conferences, trade exhibitions)
* viral marketing (use of word of mouth or Internet networking sites to spread message)
* strategic alliances (co-operation with other businesses to optimize resources).

Make your selection based on the elements that can help you achieve your goals, reach your target customers and promote your business, and which can be implemented effectively at a cost you can afford.

Consider the effectiveness of the following campaigns:

∗ A Google advertising campaign costing £1,000 could generate 5,000 clicks on your website, resulting in 200 sales at an average of £100. Your potential return is £19,000.

∗ A £500 local PR campaign to announce a new product could generate ten press mentions that in turn lead to 50 enquiries resulting in 20 sales of £100. Your potential return is £1,500.

∗ A direct mail campaign to 1,000 prospects costing £1,000 with an anticipated response rate of 3% could generate 30 customer enquires and a dozen sales of £100. Your potential return will only be £200.

Evaluate if your marketing tactics are worth the investment – are they 'nice to have' or 'must have'?

Marketing for small businesses

Here's a template of a mini marketing plan:

Heading	Contains summary of:
Situation analysis	Company, customers, collaborators, competitors, climate
Objectives	Marketing objectives (e.g. market share)
Strategies	Marketing strategies (e.g. promotion)
Tactics	Marketing tactics (e.g. advertising)
Timings	Schedule of activities
Money	Costs by activity
Labour	Human resources (e.g. in-house or outsourced)
Measures	How to evaluate the success for each campaign
Monitor	Assessment of what worked and what didn't

82

Remember to continually review your plan and the effectiveness of your campaigns. Next year, your marketing plan should be based around the successes and failures of the current activities.

Some effective marketing tactics for small businesses include:

* develop and maintain a website
* exhibit at trade shows
* create a brochure
* strategic alliances
* networking.

In small companies, networking is often a key marketing activity, enabling you to meet potential customers through informal activities such as joining networking groups, attending industry events or talking to people at business lunches.

8 Defining key messages

Communicating with your audiences

'There are four ways, and only four ways,
in which we have contact with the world.
We are evaluated and classified by these
four contacts: what we do, how we look,
what we say, and how we say it.'

Dale Carnegie

By now, you should have a good idea of how you are going
to communicate with your customers. Having identified
how, when and why, you now need to address what you
should **communicate** before deploying your campaigns.

Key messages are how you communicate with your audiences – **primarily customers but also internal teams, suppliers and shareholders**.

It is important to get the messages right to bring across the advantages of doing business with you.

These need to be **clear and consistent**, and **in line with your mission statement**. They will highlight the specific features of your products or services, and be relevant to your customers. All the information in your marketing strategy document should help you define them.

It is important to get the messages right to bring across the advantages of doing business with you

Your logo and tagline

Every business has a unique identity that is represented by a logo and often an accompanying tagline. These are the first things that customers see and they should feature on every communication and external document, from business cards and letterheads, to marketing literature and websites.

A logo is the basis of your brand and should be:

* distinctive
* eye-catching yet simple
* easy to memorize and recognize.

Good examples of logos are those of Nike and McDonalds. They have become so familiar that just part of the logo is enough to be instantly recognizable.

For small businesses, corporate identity operates on a different scale but it is still important to build brand recognition among customers.

A tagline should enhance a logo to communicate in a few words what your products or services are about. It should reflect the company's philosophy and conjure up thoughts connected to the brand without repeating the company or product name.

Consider these examples of taglines:

* Sainsbury's – 'Try something new today'
* Nike – 'Just Do It'
* Lloyds TSB – 'For the journey'
* BMW – 'The ultimate driving machine'
* Waterstones – 'What's your story?'
* Your M&S – 'This is not just food. This is M&S food.'

If considering doing business in another country, ensure that your product and company name will 'translate'. Krapp biscuits and Pschitt lemonade did not sell well when launched in the UK.

Features and benefits

Features are the characteristics of your products or services. You should have identified them when compiling your product strategy. It is important to list them so that it is clear to customers what they are.

Here are some examples of features:

* 100% fruit juice
* 24-hour service
* free delivery
* no additives or preservatives
* hand-made in Italy
* fresh produce organically grown

Features describe what is on offer. To really engage with customers and get them to understand why they should do business with you, they also need to understand the benefits.

Benefits are the features seen through the eyes of customers and should explain what they can gain from it:

* 100% fruit juice: *drinking one glass contributes to two of your five-a-day*
* 24-hour service: *you can use it whenever it suits you*
* free delivery: *it saves you the hassle of collecting and you won't be charged for it*
* no additives or preservatives: *you can safely feed it to your children*
* hand-made in Italy: *you are guaranteed the finest quality*
* fresh produce organically grown: *you won't be eating anything treated with chemicals*

Saying 'we are the best' or 'we are number one' is not a benefit. It may be the case and by all means include any industry endorsement in your literature, but only if it can be proved, such as being voted favourite retailer of the year by the leading magazine for your industry.

Testimonials and case studies

Customer feedback is great on two counts:

1 to help you understand how you are meeting your customers' expectations
2 to illustrate the reasons for doing business with you.

Customers' quotes can go a long way to act as an introduction for your business. When you get positive feedback, ask for permission to reproduce it in your marketing literature. It must be genuine and attributable to inspire confidence. For example:

> *I was delighted with the design of our website. Peter understood exactly what we were trying to achieve and delivered beyond our expectations.*

Patricia Senior, marketing director, ABC Ltd

Use quotes sparingly on your website, brochures, newsletter, blog, direct mail or PR campaigns and make sure they are relevant.

Case studies are a good way for a company to demonstrate how it has helped a customer with a specific issue. They provide a great endorsement for sales people as they help them illustrate the relevance of the product or service to a specific market segment.

Remember to:

* ask for customer feedback regularly
* conduct the occasional survey
* when you receive good feedback, ask for permission to use it.

93

The art of communication
You can't communicate with your customers and ignore your other audiences

Use internal communications to convey your company values and encourage loyalty. Keeping employees informed of what you are doing will generate trust and respect and ensure that communications with customers are effective.

Let them know when a campaign is scheduled so they are better equipped to handle queries. Share your vision and get them to embrace it. You can do this using simple and regular communications:

* an internal newsletter
* emails
* intranet (if you have one)
* meetings.

94

To ensure that your reputation grows and your messages spread, you should also communicate with other stakeholders, such as suppliers, affiliates and investors.

Marketing is at the core of the communications process but each of your audiences will interact. It is critical that your messages are consistent but delivered with the recipient in mind.

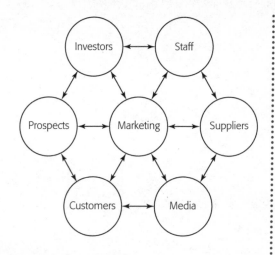

Figure 8.1: Marketing is the focal point of all communications

9 Implementing the marketing plan

Putting plans into action

Your marketing plan may include price, product, place and promotion strategies, and the tactics that you are proposing to use to achieve the objectives.

An **implementation schedule** is of vital importance to move from the conceptual to the delivery stage. Using a simple document to map out the execution process is good management and will help ensure that your marketing plan is as effective as possible.

Implementation also requires **ownership and delivery**. It is important to allocate **responsibilities** and **accountabilities**.

Small businesses may not have dedicated marketing resources. The owner or sales director will often spearhead the marketing function but the implementation itself may involve other departments.

Where a marketing function does not exist, an agency or external consultant may be sourced, but in either case it is important for **one person to co-ordinate the whole process** to ensure consistency.

An implementation schedule is of vital importance to move from the conceptual to the delivery stage

Scheduling and resourcing

Schedules

The implementation schedule for a new product launch might look like this:

Activity	Date
Marketing plan approval	May
Allocation of tasks	June
Internal communications	June
Train sales team	June
Train customer service team	June
Marketing activities start	July
External communications start	July
Update systems	July
Official launch	September
Monitor results	Ongoing
Review achievements	December
Adapt plan if required	January

Resources

* **In-house** (dedicated resource) – In-house marketing implementation provides great control over the execution of the plan; however, it implies that the company has the necessary skills and resources in place. This is often the case for larger organizations.
* **Outsourcing** (marketing agency, freelance consultant) – Outsourcing is ideal to ensure the implementation where there are no internal capabilities; as it diminishes capital investment, however, it reduces the level of control.
* **Combination** – A combination will enable you to outsource certain skills that are missing internally (such as PR or copywriting) to complement existing resources. Activities can take place more quickly while the company retains control over the overall process.

> **TOP TIP**
> With the popularity of the Internet, many resources are now available online by the hour, by the day or for however long you need them.

Key ingredients for success

Each activity in your marketing plan should contain the following information:

1 action and details – e.g. PR launch campaign to local media
2 date and duration – e.g. September and October
3 cost – e.g. £200
4 responsibility – e.g. managing director
5 resources required – e.g. freelance PR consultant
6 measure of success – e.g. five press cuttings
7 review date – e.g. November.

This will ensure:

* effective and efficient co-ordination of activities
* everybody keeps track of who is doing what and when
* outsourcing or delegation of the right activities
* monitoring of results is not overlooked.

> ### 'You can't keep doing the same thing every day and expect different results.'
> Albert Einstein

Following up on activities on a regular basis will ensure that everything is done as planned and that results are evaluated.

The absence of follow-up will almost infallibly lead to failure. Unless you know how effective your campaigns have been, you could be repeating the same errors over and over again. An effective marketing implementation also represents a competitive advantage for your business.

An effective marketing implementation also represents a competitive advantage for your business

Seizing opportunities

Collaborating with other businesses is a good idea, especially if you target the same customers with non-competing products or services. An example of this could be a marketing communications firm and a printer, or a photographer and a wedding planner.

Businesses who collaborate can split the costs of joint promotional activities, share a stand at trade exhibitions, offer discounted rates to referred customers, and list partner companies or even post a simple link on their respective websites.

104

● Combining forces to increase your reach.

CASE STUDY: An opportunity seized

The manager of an off-the-track independent petrol station, realizing that the busy station on the main road was closing down for refurbishment, placed a sign at the nearby roundabout to direct drivers to his premises. By doing so, he achieved three things:

1 provided an alternative service to drivers who would otherwise have been inconvenienced
2 created awareness of his station to an audience he could not reach before
3 increased his profits and his chances of further business from these customers.

Your marketing plan should not be set in stone. It is a working document that needs to evolve to adapt to changing market conditions.

Your marketing plan should not be set in stone...

Additional tactics

Here are some additional tactics owners of small businesses can use in their marketing plans:

* ✼ join the local chamber of commerce
* ✼ participate in relevant Business Links events
* ✼ put an offer on the back of your business cards
* ✼ offer a discount to your customers for referrals
* ✼ offer something for free on your website such as a PDF of your brochure or a newsletter
* ✼ make sure your website is optimized for search engines so your products or services can be found easily
* ✼ include a link to your website in your email signature (and for good practice on all your communications)
* ✼ attend regular 'Breakfast Club' meetings and develop relationships with other small businesses (when the need arises, they'll consider you first).

Having defined their marketing strategy and plan, the worst thing small businesses can do is fail to execute it. The implementation requires taking action, management and follow-up.

Other business imperatives may distract you from your good intentions but bear in mind that if you don't buy a lottery ticket, you will have no chance of winning.

Remember to determine:

* who owns the plan
* who is responsible for what
* dates by which activities should take place
* dates by which follow-up should take place
* measures for evaluating success.

To sum up: a good plan should be targeted, focused, easy to implement and achievable.

10 Measuring results

How to gauge success

'It is not the strongest of the species that survives, nor the most intelligent, but the one most responsive to change.'

Attributed to Charles Darwin

Predicting marketing effectiveness can seem impossible and it is sometimes difficult to evaluate performance. The overall success of a marketing plan can be measured in terms of new leads, sales or customers, increased awareness or market share; but you need to set metrics against each tactic to establish which work (or don't work) for your business.

Evaluating success may be easier for some activities but measuring the contribution of an advertising campaign can prove tricky.

There is no right or wrong way of setting metrics to evaluate effectiveness. Some companies use numbers only while others measure market perception through surveys before and after campaigns.

Taking the average response rate for your industry (for example, for an email campaign) should help you determine what would constitute a good, average or excellent response for you.

There is no right or wrong way of setting metrics to evaluate effectiveness

Investment versus return

While many businesses view **return on investment** (ROI) as a standard to measure the effectiveness of their marketing activities, it is not always possible to determine the financial contribution to the business.

A marketing campaign to generate qualified leads for the sales team should be measured against the total number of leads and not the amount of sales or revenue generated:

* measures should be set at activity level
* metrics should relate to the objective
* consider measuring values such as awareness or brand strength
* treat measurement and reporting as critical items
* upfront planning will make tracking progress easier.

Consider this example of a direct mail campaign by a financial services firm:

Objective	Generate 100 qualified sales leads
Strategy	Promotion
Tactic	Direct mail campaign to 5,000 prospects with free trial offer
Timescale	May to June
Budget	£500
Measure	Response rate: Low: 50 leads (1%) Industry average: 100 leads (2%) Good: 150 leads (3%)
Review	July to August
Results	130 leads

You can also evaluate the cost per response by dividing the budget by the number of responses and see how it compares with other activities.

If measuring ROI, bear in mind that it is down to the sales team to 'close the deal'. It is difficult to measure the value of direct mail in increasing awareness of a product.

Tracking success

Some useful tips to help you track the success of your campaigns:

✔ Make sure you have the tools in place to track results
✔ Include a unique code on each promotion
✔ Provide an incentive for prospects to quote the code (discount, free sample)
✔ Brief customer-facing teams to establish how customers found you
✔ Get every enquiry source accounted for in the contact database or on a spreadsheet
✔ If you do a customer survey, include a question on how they found you

Tracking will help the business define which tactics brought the best results and which should not be repeated. This will save invaluable time in the future.

You will then be able to concentrate on those activities that work for you and perhaps even reduce your budget or invest in other opportunities such as search engine optimization for your website or developing your social media presence.

Remember that not every activity will produce tangible results. The odd advertisement in isolation is not going to result in an abundance of enquiries. An integrated campaign, on the other hand, will help you identify which advertising channels work best.

Tracking will help the business define which tactics brought the best results and which should not be repeated

Adapting to changing markets

Over time, you may discover that what used to work no longer delivers good results. It could be a combination of market conditions and changing customer trends.

You will need to determine what has changed and adapt accordingly.

Let's consider another example. An electrical contractor using Google AdWords to promote his services achieved the following results:

	January	February	March	April	May
Impressions	561	545	578	250	268
Clicks	45	48	51	22	23

It transpired that a competing business using the same keywords had reduced his 'share of voice' on Google.

By nature, small businesses tend to be more flexible and adapt more quickly to changing market conditions than larger organizations. This means that your plan should evolve to reflect changes.

In the case of our electrical contractor, this means:

* evaluating if additional keywords are needed to refine the placement (e.g. locality)
* reviewing the ad itself and the website (it could be less appealing than that of the competitor)
* assessing if search engine optimization would be a better option (to increase natural rankings on search results).

Doing nothing is not an option. If a good source of leads has dried up, you need to assess what else you can do to compensate.

Keeping up to date

The marketing plan is not a static document but a work in progress. Having gone through the exercise once, it will be much easier next time, especially if you keep it updated.

* Once a year, you should also compile a marketing report presenting key findings.
* Review your marketing strategy document and adapt it to reflect current trends.
* Use internal communications regularly to announce successes.

Let's consider one final example – a marketing plan for a new Indian takeaway:

Tactic	Leaflets through the door with free delivery for orders within a five-mile radius
Implementation	The marketing message is right and delivered on time
Outcome	New customers start using the service
Problems	No additional staff taken on board to cope with increased order volume Late delivery, food arriving cold, no effort to compensate customer
Results	No repeat business from these customers Word of mouth means that customers relay their problems, alienating the marketing efforts

While marketing is a business function, it relies on all parts of the business for its effectiveness. The marketing plan should not be a guarded secret but a common goal for all to work together for its successful implementation.

The marketing plan is not a static document but a work in progress

Further reading

Drucker, Peter F., *Management: Tasks, Responsibilities, Practices* (HarperBusiness, 1993)

Findlay Schenck, Barbara, *Small Business Marketing for Dummies* (John Wiley & Sons, 2005)

McDonald, Malcolm & Wilson, Hugh, *Marketing Plans: How to Prepare Them, How to Use Them* (John Wiley & Sons, 2011)

Whiteling, Ian, *Online Marketing for Small Business* (Crimson Publishing, 2011)

Zaltman, Gerald, *How Customers Think: Essential Insights into the Mind of the Market* (Harvard Business School Press, 2003)

Websites

Business Link – www.businesslink.gov.uk

Small Business UK – www.smallbusinessuk.org.uk/marketing

Startups – www.startups.co.uk/marketing

A SHORT HISTORY OF MELBOURNE ARCHITECTURE

Editor: Patrick Bingham-Hall

Design: Shillington Graphics

Pesaro Publishing
PO Box 74
Balmain NSW 2041
Australia
Phone 61 2 9555 7422
Fax 61 2 9818 6999
Email pesaro@bigpond.net.au

Goad, Philip.
A Short History of Melbourne Architecture:
A Guide to Melbourne Architecture.

Includes index.
ISBN 1 877015 03 2.

1. Architecture - Victoria - Melbourne.
2. Buildings -Victoria - Melbourne.
3. Historical buildings - Victoria -Melbourne.
4. Melbourne (Vic.) - Buildings,
   structures, etc. I. Bingham-Hall, Patrick.
   II. Place, Katrina. III. Title.

720.99451

First Published in 2002 by
Pesaro Publishing, Sydney, Australia.

Photography:
Copyright © Patrick Bingham-Hall.

Text: Copyright © Philip Goad,
Katrina Place and Pesaro Publishing.

Colour Origination by
Universal Graphics, Singapore

Printed and bound by
Tien Wah Press, Singapore

*Photograph on opposite page: **Springthorpe Memorial,
Booroondara Cemetery, Kew, 1897***

*Architect - Harold Desbrowe-Annear
Sculptor - Bertram McKennal*

Introduction by
Philip Goad

Caption Text by
Katrina Place

Photography by
Patrick Bingham-Hall

A SHORT HISTORY OF MELBOURNE ARCHITECTURE

INTRODUCTION *by Philip Goad*

Melbourne's gracious public buildings and tree-lined boulevards suggest a city thoughtfully conceived, and planned with nineteenth century regard for efficient sanitation and easy access. Today, when arriving by air or by sea across the flat basin of Port Phillip Bay, the neatly defined concentration of late twentieth skyscrapers - the climactic centre to what appears to be an infinitely horizontal suburban sprawl - reinforces this perception. However, Melbourne's beginnings in 1835 were hardly grand, the township was a virtual afterthought. When pastoralists John Batman and John Pascoe Fawkner sailed up the Yarra River on independent missions to claim land, the Wurundjeri people inhabited the area. The local aboriginal people had chosen their home where the fresh, muddy brown waters of the Yarra tumbled over a small falls into a salt lagoon. It was the perfect place to moor ships and to obtain fresh drinking water. A transaction between Batman and Wurundjeri elders appeared to secure the land for the land-hunters from Van Diemen's Land (Tasmania), even though the settlement, in fact all pastoral occupation of Victoria, was considered illegal by the colonial administration in Sydney. In response, Captain William Lonsdale was sent in October 1836 to the Port Phillip District of New South Wales, as it was then known, to survey the area, lay out the town plan and the surrounding land, and sell off the land to the highest bidders. In 1837, Robert Hoddle laid out the town reserve just north of the lagoon. This was the first part of the city's now distinctive grid plan: 24 ten acre square blocks, in three rows of eight, each block bounded by major streets and bisected by narrow streets running east-west. This grid, bounded by Flinders, Spring, Lonsdale and Spencer Streets, was aligned carefully to take in the natural features of the site, two small hills (to the east and the west), a creek (still running today under Elizabeth Street), and an escarpment to the west.

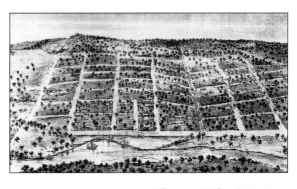

*'Melbourne in 1838 from the Yarra Yarra'
from the La Trobe Collection,
State Library of Victoria.*

The modest township was named after the British Prime Minister, Viscount Melbourne.

The first buildings in Melbourne were modest: tents, and bark and timber slab huts. Some of the earliest forms of permanent shelter were prefabricated. John Batman himself erected a prefabricated timber house on what became known as Batman's Hill. Superintendent Charles Joseph La Trobe arrived in 1839, and brought a small cottage manufactured by John Manning of London. Uniform panels for standard doors, windows and wall sections were slotted between evenly spaced timber posts. Other materials suitable for prefabrication were corrugated iron and cast iron, and the practice of erecting portable buildings for residences, commercial buildings, and even churches, continued into the early 1850s.

Williamstown Lighthouse, 1848
Battery Road, Williamstown
Architect - Henry Ginn (Public Works Department)

Melbourne soon gained a series of substantial buildings, despite the recession of the early 1840s. St. James's (Anglican) Cathedral (1839-51) was constructed from local sandstone, and designed by Robert Russell who had been part of a survey team sent to Melbourne in 1835, returning in 1838 as a Clerk of Works in the Colonial Architect's office. The distinctive building material that came into favour during the 1840s was bluestone, the grey/blue basalt found in the country west of the town. The bluestone lighthouse at Williamstown (1848) is one of the very few buildings that survive from the Colonial Architect's office under Henry Ginn. Several large houses like 'Como', South Yarra (1846,1854) and 'Bishopscourt', East Melbourne (1849-51), appeared outside the township in new suburbs and on some of the larger agricultural estates created to the east of Melbourne near the Yarra. These houses embodied a Picturesque sensibility, employing Regency, Italianate, and Mediaeval styles. Melbourne was beginning to take shape.

In 1851, the State of Victoria was formed. This brought separation from the colonial administration of New South Wales and new focus to the six-year old township of 23,000 people. Change would be doubly significant that year, when gold was discovered in Ballarat. Almost overnight, Melbourne ballooned in size, wealth and population. The town became a city. Over the next three decades, it gained its own parliament house, a public library, a university, a post office, a town hall, and two new

Old Treasury Building 1858-62, Spring Street, Melbourne Architect - JJ Clark(Public Works Department)

cathedrals, amongst a host of other new institutions such as gaols, law courts, hospitals and a lunatic asylum. It also gained splendid public gardens like the Fitzroy Gardens and the Royal Botanic Gardens. Above all, it gained urbanity.

Emblematic of Melbourne's irresistible rise were the Treasury Building (1858-62), and the Royal Mint (1869-72). Designed in the Renaissance Revival style by JJ Clark, they signified Victoria's newfound political and economic independence. This restrained palazzo idiom would characterise Melbourne's city streets in the 1860s and 1870s, and be popular as the preferred style for gentlemen's clubs, banks, shops, and in the hands of

See Yup Temple, 1866
76 Raglan Street, South Melbourne
Architect - George Wharton

an architect like Leonard Terry, the most elegant of warehouses. In the surrounding suburbs, speculators constructed rows of workers cottages and terrace houses. Those who continued to benefit from the Gold Rush commissioned larger and more elaborate villas. Of all of these, it was the picturesque Italianate forms of Government House (1872-76) in the Kings Domain that would be the pacesetter of taste for Melbourne's upper class. Across the suburbs, the recipe of asymmetrical massing, projecting window bays, a tower, low hipped roofs, and plain stuccoed walls became the norm for large houses set upon Melbourne's sprinkling of hills, and the aspiration for the most humble cottage.

The Gold Rush (1851-61) also highlighted Melbourne's different cultures. Larger synagogues and numerous churches were built, such as George Wharton's See Yup Temple, South Melbourne (1866) for the city's Cantonese migrants. Between 1851 and 1881, Melbourne grew more than twenty times its size. With its growth, came the establishment of substantial architectural practices, such as Reed and Barnes, founded in 1852 by Joseph Reed, who were to design many of Melbourne's most important churches and public buildings. Another significant practice was the Victorian Public Works Department. From 1858 for twenty years, William

Wardell steered this influential office, while at the same time designing Pugin inspired Gothic Revival churches, including the great bluestone St Patrick's Cathedral (1858-1940).

If the 1870s had been prosperous years for Melbourne, the 1880s represented the zenith of its economic and political power. Wealth and individualism characterised its society and its buildings. 'Marvellous Melbourne' became a metropolis of global pretension. Before its ignominious fall from grace with the depression between 1891 and 1893, Melbourne could boast a cable tram network that was one of the largest in the world; one of the world's tallest buildings with Oakden Addison and Kemp's Australia Building (1888, demolished); and a series of suburban town halls, each more elaborate, florid and exuberant than the one before.

In architectural terms, the city came to define its own historical style – Boom

St Patrick's Cathedral, 1858-1940, Gisborne Street, Melbourne
Architect - William Wardell

Rialto Building, 1889
497 Collins Street, Melbourne
Architect - William Pitt

Style – where the Italianate and the Renaissance Revival were elaborated to Baroque dimensions. In the hands of architects such as Twentyman and Askew, William Pitt, and JAB Koch, the façades of banks, department stores, offices, and coffee palaces were given ever richer and more sophisticated overlays of trabeated and arcuated classical schemes. These included giant classical orders, balustraded parapets, cement-rendered swags and festoons of fruit, and entire compositions that expanded through decorative repetition and the addition of Mannerist clock towers and mansard domes. Central Melbourne also grew its own Gothic Revival streetscape bookended by the Olderfleet and Rialto Buildings (1889) at the western end of Collins Street; it was a 19th century fantasy on mercantile Venice. On Spring Street at the other end of the city, the Windsor Hotel (1884-88) and Princess Theatre (1886-87) suggested the grand pavilioned palaces of Second Empire Paris. Out in the suburbs, mansions such as 'Illawarra' (1888-89), 'Stonington' (1891) and 'Labassa' (1889-91) demonstrated similar unequalled sumptuousness. It is a period maligned for its decadence and occasional vulgarity, but the dexterity and exuberance of its architecture has yet to be fully appreciated.

If the interregnum of recession put an end to Melbourne's cavort with an architecture of excess, the city's architecture culture did not rest. Prior to the crash, the architectural qualities of red brick and bright orange terracotta roof tiles were seen in houses like 'North Park', Essendon (1889) and 'Tay Creggan', Hawthorn (1892). With public buildings like Kew Court House (1886-88) and the Austral Buildings in Collins Street (1891), English Queen Anne Revival and vernacular Free Style ideas were introduced. Arts and Crafts influences from Great Britain and the United States were explored as local architects argued in their professional journals as to what might constitute an

'Tay Creggan', 1892
30 Yarra Street, Hawthorn
Architect - Guyon Purchas

appropriate Australian style of architecture. Truthfulness to materials and an ethic of morality associated with the Gothic Revival lay behind this move towards a gradual rejection of the Classical styles, and the acceptance of exposed textures, natural 'earth' colours, and a compositional technique of radical eclecticism that would emerge from the mid-1890s. The leading innovators were Robert Haddon, Harold Desbrowe-Annear, Rodney Alsop and Walter Butler. While Australia's Federation in 1901 has been proposed as the cause of this shift towards an apparently self-grown aesthetic idiom, it was actually the centenary in 1888 of the first European settlement that brought about a new self-consciousness and encouraged architects to talk of an Australian style. As early as 1882, Melbourne architect Nahum Barnet had argued for a 'Climatic Architecture' specifically suited to Australian conditions.

The almost complete shift by 1905 to a new domestic style, the so-called Queen Anne, was assisted by Melbourne's rapid suburban growth and the expansion of its rail and electric tram lines. In Malvern, Essendon, and Albert Park, a handful of firms, notably the partnership of Beverley Ussher and Henry Kemp, realised a new idealised picturesque villa. Its image was not Italianate, but firmly rooted in the Arts and Crafts: red brick walls and tall chimneys, turned timber posts, roughcast render, half-timbered gable ends, return verandahs, dominating hip roofs, and terracotta roof tiles.

Federation brought a new aspiration to the southern city. Between 1901 and 1926, Melbourne was the temporary capital of Australia. As if realising the city's opportunity to parade itself as a re-born ornament of empire, buildings like Flinders Street Railway Station (1901-11), the City Baths (1904), and the Spencer Street Mail Exchange (1917), embraced the imperial forms of the Edwardian Baroque. When final plans for the new capital, Canberra, were formally announced in 1911, its designers the Chicago-based architects Walter Burley Griffin and Marion Mahony settled in Melbourne. They soon gained commissions and challenged conservative clients with such buildings as Newman College (1915-18), and for enlightened patrons, a series of Prairie-style houses and innovative subdivision designs for Eaglemont, Keilor and Mount Eliza.

After World War I, Melbourne's architectural qualities shifted again, but in more subtle ways. The speculative house success of the 1920s was the bungalow. Roof pitches dropped to reflect a Japanese influence disseminated through the Californian

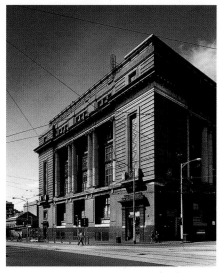

Spencer Street Mail Exchange, 1917
164-200 Spencer Street, Melbourne
Architect - John Smith Murdoch
(Commonwealth Department of Works)

bungalow. There were clinker bricks, low front fences with privet hedges, buffalo grass lawns, and sleeping porches with roll-down blinds. The 1920s also experienced a plethora of period revival styles, from Georgian, Tudor, French Provincial, and the popular Spanish Mission, that were not just applied to houses but also to the growing number of flats and apartments in suburbs like South Yarra and St. Kilda.

Nicholas Building, 1926
27-41 Swanston Street, Melbourne
Architect - Harry Norris

American presence was also felt in the city with two great monuments to the new public entertainment medium of film. Griffin and Mahony's Capitol Theatre, which opened in 1924, had a fantastic plaster crystalcave/auditorium, and the Moorish fantasy of the State Theatre (1928, now The Forum), had an interior designed to simulate sitting outdoors with a Mediterranean blue night sky overhead. The central city consolidated in density as buildings were restricted by the 40 metre (132 feet) height limit, which was conducive to the new form of office building, the commercial palazzo. Faced in Wunderlich's 'Granitex' faience (glazed terracotta tile), The Nicholas Building (1926) epitomised the new type. Built to maximum site coverage, it had a massive base with shops and arcade at ground level, a shaft of offices, and an elaborate attic story and gigantic cornice. During the 1920s and early 1930s, the city acquired many such buildings in Modern Gothic, Spanish, and Modern Georgian styles.

Outside the central business district, City Beautiful ideals of the 1920s led to the flamboyant Church Street Bridge (1920-24), the City Engineer's dainty Spanish style Conservatory (1929) in the Fitzroy Gardens, and most significantly, the tree-planting of Royal Parade, Flemington Parade, Victoria Parade and St Kilda Road. The Shrine of Remembrance (1927-34), axially located and a sober memorial to the Great War, was to become Melbourne's most important public monument, a focus of cultural identity that balanced the monumental scale of Melbourne's colonial grid plan across the northern side of the Yarra. Melbourne's last architectural hurrah before the Depression took hold in 1929 was not a monument but an office building. The Modern Gothic pinnacles of the Manchester Unity Building (1929-32) made it the tallest building in Melbourne. The Moderne towers of commerce had outstripped the city's steeples.

In the 1930s, Melbourne's architectural profession was committed to tasteful architectural manners and a concern for 'street architecture', where buildings respected the line of the street,

Conservatory, Fitzroy Gardens, 1929
East Melbourne
Architect - MCC City Engineer's Department

and were given non-intrusive silhouettes and restrained surface modulation. At the same time, they embraced not just the glamorous streamlined forms of the Moderne, but also the new functionalist architecture of European Modernism. In the Dandenong Ranges east of the city, prolific commercial architect Harry Norris designed 'Burnham Beeches' (1933) for Aspro mogul Alfred Nicholas, a vast three-storey 'Xanadu in Jazz' built of reinforced concrete and studded with diamond motifs representing Australian animals.

'Burnham Beeches', 1933
Sherbrooke Road, Sassafras
Architect - Harry Norris

It was 1934, Melbourne's centenary year, that brought Melbourne's architecture culture into focus. Norman Seabrook's design for MacRobertson Girls High School, was a meticulously detailed composition of cream brick prisms relieved by blue glazed brick sills and vermilion steel window frames. Inspired by the Dutch architect Willem Dudok, this school was a direct challenge to the prevailing sobriety of official government architecture. Even more challenging were the startling cantilevered

Mercy Hospital, 1934-36
Grey Street, East Melbourne
Architect - Stephenson & Meldrum

concrete balconies of the Mercy (1934-36) and Freemasons (1936) hospitals in East Melbourne, both designed by Stephenson and Meldrum. With these uncompromising examples of a new idiom of sanatoria found in Finland and Switzerland, the architecture of health signalled the way for new representations of the town hall, the office building, the apartment block, the church, and the factory. By 1943, even the image of the law had changed, with the Russell Street Police Headquarters (1940-43) realised as a stepped Gotham City profiled skyscraper.

Political turmoil in Europe had caused migration from the mid-1930s onward, and Melbourne, like all Australian capital cities, was the beneficiary of talented émigré

'Glenunga', 1941
2 Horsburgh Grove, Armadale
Architect - Romberg & Shaw

architects. Chief among them was Frederick Romberg, who with Mary Turner Shaw, designed two influential apartment blocks, 'Glenunga' in Armadale (1941) and 'Newburn' in Queens Road, Melbourne (1939-42). His most significant work was the high-rise block, 'Stanhill' (1945-50), also in Queens Road, a compositional tour-de-force in reinforced concrete and glass that echoed the dynamic forms of German Expressionist Erich Mendelsohn, and the humanistic detail of Finnish Modernist, Alvar Aalto.

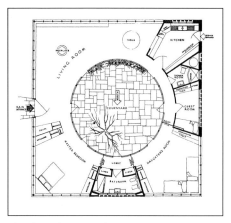

Plan of Grounds House, 1954
24 Hill Street, Toorak
Architect - Roy Grounds

World War 2 curtailed construction and enabled time for reassessment. In the postwar decade, Melbourne's architecture culture reinvented itself, now wholly self-conscious in its confidence. Robin Boyd described 1950s Melbourne as Australia's "cradle of modernity". After years of postwar austerity and failed attempts to relieve the postwar housing shortage through prefabrication schemes, the prospect of an Olympic Games in 1956 galvanised the city towards experiment. The single-family house became the focus of the most concerted architectural energies. Daring structural experiments with curving corrugated concrete shells and cantilevering steel, coupled with Platonic planning shapes, inspired the rationale for houses by Robin Boyd, Peter and Dione McIntyre, and Kevin Borland. Roy Grounds took pure geometries as his cue for houses with perfect square, circular and triangular plans. His own house (1954) in Toorak with its square plan and circular courtyard was a miniature precursor to his much larger National Gallery of Victoria (1961-68).

The two most dramatic buildings of the decade were the Olympic Swimming Stadium (1952-56, now altered) and the recently restored Sidney Myer Music Bowl (1956-59).

Both feats of engineering dexterity, the former was a taut glazed shed tied down to the ground; and the latter a metallic canopy draped from two cigar-shaped pylons. These buildings, though singular in their conception, were not the only forms of postwar monumentality, there was interest in the crafted Scandinavian good taste that would characterise university buildings throughout the 1950s, and a revived appreciation of the work of Frank Lloyd Wright after his death in 1959. By the mid-1960s, however, there was a complete reaction to the previous decade.

In came a celebration of exposed materials and natural textures, a vernacular approach, a deliberate enclosure of private space by solid rather than transparent walls, and a predilection for off-form concrete as a more tangible expression of humanity.

In the 1960s, Melbourne's central city reached for the sky following the historic breaking of the height limit in 1958 by ICI House. The skyscraper reached its aesthetic climax with the Miesian elegance of BHP House (1967-72). Out in Melbourne's suburbs, there could be glimpsed different preoccupations. McGlashan and Everist's house for John and Sunday Reed, Heide II (1966), described at the time by Neil Clerehan as "International Style set down amongst the melaleucas", was a marvellous live-in stone

Museum of Modern Art at Heide (Heide II), 1966
7 Templestowe Road, Bulleen
Architect - McGlashan & Everist

garden maze. This was one of the last truly formalist exercises of orthodox Modernism in Melbourne before a younger generation promoted an entirely different way of considering architecture. Angles in plan, form, and roofline became the new signs of being up-to-date.

By the mid-1970s, the city was shunned by all except the large corporate firms. As stages for architectural production, Melbourne's city and its bush periphery seemed polar opposites, with the suburbs as a cultural no-man's land in between. The rise of the heritage movement and its protests against the destruction of Collins Street, the building of new freeways, and the decimation of the inner suburbs by the Victorian Housing Commission slum clearance scheme, suggested crisis within the local Melbourne scene.

Plumbers and Gasfitters Union Building, 1970
52 Victoria Street, Melbourne
Architect - Graeme Gunn

Architects like Kevin Borland, Graeme Gunn, Daryl Jackson and Evan Walker devoted themselves to the design of project housing, schools, community and trade union buildings.

A new generation of Melbourne architects, spearheaded by Peter Corrigan, began to argue for the relevance of the suburbs. This position was rare in Australia. Corrigan, with Maggie Edmond, challenged all architectural

conventions with a series of churches and schools. Ugly and ordinary architecture was alright, and it was driven by an ethic of non-pretension and a hope for the collective spirit. Work by others such as Norman Day, Peter Crone and Greg Burgess celebrated the return of architectural artifice. Edmond and Corrigan, Crone, and Burgess all participated in the Ministry of Housing's Kay Street housing development, Carlton (1981-83). Their response was not slum clearance but contextually responsible townhouse infill. They engaged with the city and its history. In the central city and the inner suburbs, such buildings as No. 1 Collins Street (1983), MacRae and Way Studio (1985), and the Brunswick Community Health Care Centre (1985-90) employed witty, and even ironic, references to context. Melbourne had earned the imprimatur of the postmodern city.

The mid-1980s saw Melbourne boom again and numerous office towers were commissioned before another stockmarket crash in 1987. Towers such as 101 Collins Street (1986-90), Shell House (1988), Telstra Corporate Centre

101 Collins Street, 1990
Architect - Denton Corker Marshall

(1989-92), and 120 Collins Street (1991) were the symbols of the new corporate revival and the boom, albeit hollow, in office building. When that came to an end, the university literally came to town. RMIT University, encouraged by Professor Leon van Schaik, contributed a series of innovative buildings to the city. The two best known are Edmond and Corrigan's postmodern masterpiece RMIT Building 8 (1991-94) and Ashton Raggatt McDougall's encrusted green, purple, and intensely symbolically coded, Storey Hall (1995). Then, filling the vacuum created by the dearth of office building, there came a new form of urban consolidation: the re-housing of the city. The Boom Style of the 1880s returned in the form of Nonda Katsalidis' exuberant architectural cocktails which included sculptures, serrated fins, and totemic towers of apartments. His Melbourne Terraces (1994), Silos Apartments (1996), and Republic Tower (2000) signalled a rebirth of Melbourne's tradition of architectural formalism.

In total contrast to the socially conscious years of the 1970s, an 'edifice' complex settled in through the late 1990s with the Liberal State Government of Jeff Kennett. The Crown Casino (1993-97) was built to raise government revenue, and 'Agenda 21', the government's politically charged programme of major civic monuments, was implemented. Included amongst a host of heritage-based projects were an Exhibition Centre (1996), the new CityLink gateway to Melbourne (1999), and the Melbourne Museum (2001), all designed by Denton Corker Marshall, and Federation Square (1997-2002) designed by LAB Architects in association with Bates Smart.

Bereft of determining landscape and demanding climate, Melbourne's architects have always revelled in the artifice of architecture and formal experiment. The city possesses many architecture cultures, all simultaneously offering opinions on what might constitute an appropriate architecture for the city. In the past eight years, an entirely new generation of Melbourne architectural firms has emerged. The work of Wood Marsh, for example, aspires to Land Art, gorgeous materiality, and the patina of silent age. Their buildings are not so much concerned with climate or structure, as with sensual and formal reverie. University buildings, houses, and apartment designs now provide the richest lode for architectural experiment. It could be said that Melbourne's pluralistic culture has no focus. However such an opinion underestimates the positive attributes of an intense self-awareness of Melbourne's architectural history, the quality of its streets, its grid, its gardens, and its often wayward and obsessive preoccupation with ideas. There is a corresponding intensity to

Building C, Deakin University, 1996
Burwood Highway, Burwood
Architect - Wood Marsh with
Pels Innes Neilson & Kosloff

its history of architecture that is matched by the city's volatility in the face of economic fortune. For as a local poet writing under the name 'Melbourne Juvenal' said in the late 1880s:

"Ours is a city ever in extremes
Or in a nightmare or in golden dreams."

1839-51

St James's Old Cathedral

Originally located in Collins Street, St James's Cathedral was Melbourne's first Anglican church. The design of the church, constructed from local sandstone, was influenced by the work of Francis Greenway. The octagonal tower, side porches and the east (now north) end were designed by Charles Laing. The church was relocated to King Street in 1913.

419-435 King Street, Melbourne

Architect - Robert Russell

Corrugated Iron Houses, South Melbourne 1853

The three portable pre-fabricated houses located at this site are evocative of Melbourne's pre gold-rush history. Only one, the 6-room attic cottage facing the street, is original to the site, the others were moved there in the 1970s and 1980s. The second house, relocated from Fitzroy, was constructed according to a patent by Edward Bellhouse of Manchester and is possibly the only one of its kind remaining in the world.

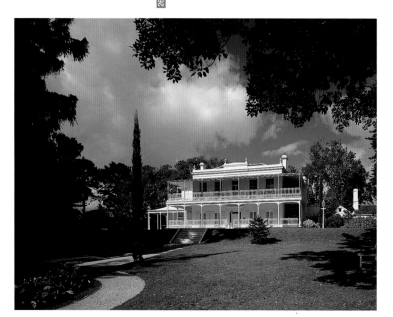

1854 *'Como', South Yarra*

The elegant Regency form of 'Como' was an extension to an earlier house (1846), located on a block of land extending to the Yarra River. Palisade iron railings and gates, shipped out from Scotland, were added later, as was a ballroom by architect AE Johnson, when the Armytage family purchased 'Como' in the 1870s. The house, named after Lake Como in Italy, remains a monument to mid-Victorian social life.

Como Avenue, South Yarra   *Architect Unknown*

State Library of Victoria **1854**

The State Library, founded by Sir Redmond Barry and designed in the Roman Revival style, was also once home to the National Gallery and the National Museum. In 1906-11, Bates Peebles and Smart added a reading room, the dome of which was the largest reinforced concrete dome in the world at the time. The 1990s extensions on La Trobe and Russell Streets were designed by Ancher Mortlock and Woolley.

304-328 Swanston Street, Melbourne   *Architect - Joseph Reed*

1856 *Corio Villa, Geelong*

The ornate cast-iron pieces, roofing iron, and vases which comprise Corio Villa were ordered from Charles D Young & Co of Edinburgh by William Nairn Grey, the Commission for Crown Lands for the Portland Bay District. Grey died before he could take possession, and the components were instead purchased by Alfred Douglas, who had it erected without supervisory plans or directions.

56 Eastern Beach Road, Geelong

Parliament House 1856

Peter Kerr's grand Roman Revival design created a dramatic termination to Bourke Street. The building, which contains some of Australia's most refined 19th century interiors, was built in a piecemeal fashion and remains unfinished, its dome yet to be constructed. The building was added to many times, including the library (1859-1861), Queen's Hall (1877-1879) and the grand western façade (1879-1892).

Spring Street, Melbourne   *Architect - Knight & Kerr*

1857 *Clarendon Terrace, East Melbourne*

Clarendon Terrace was one of Melbourne's most sought after residential addresses.
The houses formed a row of three terraces, united visually by a grand giant order Corinthian
portico which rose the height of the stucco building. The architect, Osgood Pritchard also
designed the adjacent 206 Clarendon Street, a similarly gracious Italianate building.

208-212 Clarendon Street, East Melbourne   *Architect - Osgood Pritchard*

Royal Terrace, Fitzroy 1858

Attributed to architect John Gill, the bluestone (Victorian basalt) row of terraces is one of the largest and oldest in Melbourne. Located on elevated land opposite the Royal Exhibition Building and Gardens, the terraces were designed for a wealthy upper-middle class clientele, with living rooms on the ground floor, and bedrooms on the upper two levels.

Nicholson and Gertrude Streets, Fitzroy   *Architect - John Gill*

1861

Hodgkinson House, East Melbourne

Clement Hodgkinson was Assistant Commissioner of the Lands and Survey Department when this bluestone home in the Gothic Revival style was built. It was an unusual choice of style for an inner-suburban home, and is notable for the decorative turned timberwork on the verandahs. Hodgkinson was responsible for the laying out of a number of parks and gardens, including the Treasury, Fitzroy, and Flagstaff Gardens.

157 Hotham Street, East Melbourne

Architect - Joseph Reed

Old Treasury Building 1858-62

The architect, JJ Clark, was only nineteen years old when he completed the elegant Renaissance Revival design of the Treasury Building. A draftsman in the Public Works Department, he took his design from the form of a 16th century Italian palazzo. The building was designed to hold gold bullion in basement strongrooms, beneath a floor one metre thick.

Spring Street, Melbourne   *Architect – JJ Clark (Public Works Department)*

1841-64

Old Melbourne Gaol

Before the construction of the Old Melbourne Gaol, the city's growing criminal population was housed in a variety of venues, including stockades in Richmond, Collingwood, and Pentridge, and in hulks moored off Williamstown. The design was based on the work of English prison engineer, Joshua Jebb. The present cell block housed about 170 prisoners and witnessed 104 hangings, including that of Ned Kelly in 1880. The Gaol was closed in 1929.

Russell and Franklin Streets, Melbourne   *Architect Unknown*

1859-67

Melbourne General Post Office

The imposition of trabeated classical orders of architecture onto an arcuated structure created one of Melbourne's most refined Renaissance Revival forms. The Melbourne General Post Office was built to the design of AE Johnson, of Smith & Johnson. Originally two storeys high, a third storey and a tower were added in 1885-90, and further extensions were made on Elizabeth Street in 1907.

Corner Elizabeth Street and Bourke Street, Melbourne

Architect – Smith & Johnson
(Public Works Department)

1867 *St Michael's Church*

On the site of the first permanent church in Melbourne (1839), the former Independent Church was designed in the Lombardic Romanesque style and was one of the first Melbourne buildings to employ polychrome brickwork. The Romanesque interior was designed as a sloping ampitheatre with an upper gallery. St Michael's acts as a foil to the scholarly Scots Church opposite, also designed by Joseph Reed in 1873.

Corner of Collins Street and Russell Street, Melbourne   *Architect - Reed & Barnes*

'Rippon Lea', Elsternwick **1868**

The original 15-room polychrome mansion was designed for Frederick Sargood in the Lombardic Romanesque style. 'Rippon Lea' was extended continually over 30 years to comprise 33 rooms, and sat within extensive and elaborate gardens totaling 43 acres. Much of the land has been sold off, and ten acres remain today. The original ballroom was replaced in the 1930s, and many of the interiors were redecorated.

192 Hotham Street, Elsternwick   *Architect - Reed & Barnes*

1858-69
St Patrick's Cathedral

St Patrick's Cathedral is the largest church building in Victoria, and one of the world's largest Gothic Revival churches. Wardell's design, constructed from Footscray bluestone, was influenced by both English and French Gothic architecture. It was not finally completed until 1940, with the construction of the three spires. Wardell had designed over thirty churches in England before he migrated to Australia in 1858.

5 Gisborne Street, Melbourne   *Architect - William Wardell*

1870

Melbourne Town Hall

The French Renaissance style Melbourne Town Hall was the prototype for the numerous town halls which were erected in Melbourne's suburbs in the late 19th century. This exuberant composition, faced in Tasmanian freestone above a bluestone plinth, results from numerous additions and extensions by Reed & Barnes, ending with the 1928 extension along Collins Street, designed by Stephenson & Meldrum with A & K Henderson

90-130 Swanston Street, Melbourne

Architect - Reed and Barnes

1872
Former Royal Mint

Designed in the manner of an Italian Renaissance palazzo, the Royal Mint was built to mint the gold pouring in from Victoria's gold fields. Despite receiving instructions to design a plain building without ornamentation, JJ Clark's modifications of a plan drawn up in London are remarkably elegant and sophisticated. The Royal Mint closed in 1968.

280-318 William Street, Melbourne

Architect -JJ Clark (Public Works Department)

Government House 1872-76

Located within 11 hectares of grounds adjacent to the Royal Botanic Gardens, Government House rises majestically above a thick canopy of trees. William Wardell's Italianate design was inspired by Osborne House on the Isle of Wight, and consists of the State Ballroom, the State Rooms, and the Vice-Regal apartments. Between 1901 and 1926, Government House was home to the governors-general of Australia.

Government House Drive, The King's Domain, Melbourne

Architect – William Wardell
(Public Works Department)

1878 *Mandeville Hall, Toorak*

Webb extended an existing 12 room house, 'St Georges' (1867), into the 30 room mansion 'Athelstane' for Joseph Clarke, creating one of Melbourne's grandest Boom-style mansions. Externally the colonnaded balconies of the mansion proclaimed Clarke's wealth, whilst internally the house was given lavish new decorations by Gillow & Co, London. 'Athelstane' became Mandeville Hall, a private school for girls, in 1924.

10 Mandeville Crescent, Toorak   *Architect - Charles Webb*

Werribee Park Mansion 1873-1878

Werribee Park was built for the Scottish pastoralist brothers, Thomas and Andrew Chirnside. The symmetrical Italianate homestead was erected as a showpiece with gardens laid out by William Guilfoyle. The Chirnside brothers had a troubled relationship, as both wished to marry their first cousin. Thomas later committed suicide. Werribee Park was purchased by the Roman Catholic Church and extended in 1923 for use as a seminary.

South Drive, Werribee   *Architect - James Henry Fox*

1880

Melbourne Exhibition Building

The Exhibition Buildings originally covered a 60 acre site for the 1888 Melbourne Centennial Exhibition. Only the central building remains, with a dome inspired by Brunelleschi's Duomo in Florence rising above the intersection of the transept and the long nave. The lavish internal decoration of the dome and its supporting arches contrasts with the utilitarian timber struts and iron roof of the nave.

Carlton Gardens, Carlton

Architect - Reed & Barnes

South Melbourne Town Hall 1880

The former Emerald Hill Town Hall is comprised of giant Corinthian columned and pilastered pavilion bays flanking a central portico. The height of the clocktower has been exaggerated by the removal of mansarded towers and of the urns which lined the parapets. A stately urban space on Bank Street was created in 1928 with the construction of the Spanish Mission style Courthouse and Police Station opposite, designed by E Evan Smith.

208-220 Bank Street, South Melbourne   *Architect - Charles Webb*

1880

St George's Church, St Kilda

St George's was a scholarly interpretation of a polychromatic brick English Gothic Revival church. The design encompasses a double-gabled entrance porch adjacent to a soaring slim banded bell tower. The porch is topped by a triangular rose window. Internally the space is unusual, with a hall-like T-shaped plan, an absence of aisles, a sloping floor, and broad transepts and walls detailed with red and cream brick.

4 Chapel Street, St Kilda

Architect - Albert Purchas

1881

Ormond College, University of Melbourne

Ormond College, a refined Gothic Revival building in an overtly English university tradition, is built from rough-hewn Barrabool sandstone on a bluestone plinth with cream brick dressings around the windows and doors. The College, based around a cloistered quadrangle, was erected by the Presbyterian Church and substantially funded by Francis Ormond. The tower is a landmark seen from the University, Parkville, and Royal Parade.

University of Melbourne, College Crescent, Parkville   *Architect - Reed & Barnes*

1884

Former E S & A Bank

The Venetian Gothic banking chambers, built from Pyrmont (Sydney) sandstone, were designed for the bank's general manager, Sir George Verdon, and are acknowledged as one of the prolific Wardell's finest works. The Queen Street façade is a lyrical reworking of the loggia from the Doge's Palace in Venice. A lavish High-Victorian interior features cast-iron columns with wrought-copper capitals of flowers, leaves, and vegetables.

390 Collins Street, Melbourne

Architect - William Wardell

Princess Theatre 1887

Designed in the French Second Empire style in a pavilion plan, the Princess Theatre is emblematic of the 'Boom Style', with three mansard roof domes adorned with cast-iron lace crowns and a winged female trumpeter. A stained-glass wintergarden was added in the 1920s. The design of the theatre was a great technological breakthrough, as it resolved an ongoing problem of ventilating a packed theatre.

163-181 Spring Street, Melbourne   *Architect - William Pitt*

1884-88 *Windsor Hotel*

The Windsor Hotel, with its twin French Second Empire towers and opulent interiors, is one of Australia's most majestic 19th century hotels. Built with 200 rooms in 1884 and known as the Grand Hotel, it was extended for the Centenary Exhibition of 1888 to 360 rooms, and named the Grand Coffee Palace in the spirit of temperance of the time. It was renamed the Windsor Hotel in the 1920s.

137 Spring Street, Melbourne   *Architect - Charles Webb*

Prince's Bridge **1888**

A competition-winning design of three segmental iron girder arches, Prince's Bridge was the third to cross the Yarra River at this location, replacing the original timber bridge and a subsequent arched stone bridge. A noteworthy adornment to this sober and dignified crossing is the placement of the coats of arms of municipal and governmental authorities (who funded the bridge) within the spandrel panels above the low arches.

St Kilda Road, Melbourne   *Architect - Jenkins D'Ebro & Grainger*

1888

Sum Kum Lee General Store

Built for Chinese merchant Lowe Kong Meng for use as business premises, a warehouse and as a 'first-class residence', the Baroque massing and Mannerist details were more typical of a larger building, rather than a narrow urban building thoroughly enclosed by its surroundings. Though generally occupied by Chinese groceries and restaurants, the building was owned for a short time, c. 1903, by Maurice Brodsky, the controversial journalist and publisher of Table Talk.

112-114 Little Bourke Street, Melbourne

Architect - George De Lacy Evans

1889

'Illawarra', Toorak

'Illawarra' was built just before the stockmarket crash of 1893 for the colourful politician and landboomer Charles Henry James. The mansion is an opulent mix of Mannerist classical details, vernacular rooflines and picturesque composition, with a landmark tower worthy of a town hall. Its forms can be seen as a forerunner to the Queen Anne Revival which would sweep across Melbourne at the turn of the century.

1 Illawarra Crescent, Toorak

Architect - James Birtwhistle

1889

Olderfleet Building

William Pitt designed the Olderfleet Building and the neighbouring Rialto Building, bookending a spectacular mercantile streetscape of five buildings, for Patrick McCaughlan in 1889. The Olderfleet is a four-storey Venetian Gothic building with an ornate Ruskinian façade topped by a pinnacled Gothic Revival clock tower. The spandrels above the pointed Gothic arches of the windows are inlaid with decorative tiles.

477 Collins Street, Melbourne   *Architect - William Pitt*

1889

The Rialto Building

The Rialto Building gained both its name and its stylistic derivative from 16th century Venice, and was designed to house a complex of offices and warehouses. Based on the Gothic palazzo, the design features coloured tiles, polychromatic banding, pointed arches and columnettes. When the building was connected to a new hotel in 1980 to become Le Meridien at Rialto, the internal balconies and the cobbled laneway were retained in an atrium.

503 Collins Street, Melbourne

Architect - William Pitt

1890

Fitzroy Town Hall

WJ Ellis began the Fitzroy Town Hall, designing the hall wing and first tower in 1873. The remainder of the Roman Revival building was completed in 1890 by George Johnson, one of Victoria's most prolific public architects. Externally, the town hall is dominated by two monumental flights of steps leading to Roman Corinthian porticoes. The building contains a much revered double-height library.

201 Napier Street, Fitzroy

Architect - George Johnson

St Paul's Cathedral 1880-91

St Paul's Cathedral is one the largest built works of the English Gothic Revival architect William Butterfield, who never visited Australia. Built in contrasting 'polytexture' sandstone, the Cathedral was not completed to Butterfield's design, as the spires are not his, they were designed by James Barr, and built in 1926-31. The adjacent Chapter House and Diocesan Offices, also in the Gothic Revival style, are to Butterfield's design.

2 Swanston Street, Melbourne   *Architect - William Butterfield*

1891

Former A C Goode House

The Adelaide-based practice of Wright Reed & Beaver took their inspiration from the French Gothic Revival style for the National Mutual Life Association Building (later A C Goode House, now the Bank of New Zealand). The flamboyant Gothic exterior is matched by colourful and richly detailed interior spaces. The eastern Queen Street façade was extended by 24 metres in 1903.

389-399 Collins Street, Melbourne

Architect - Wright Reed & Beaver

1891

Block Arcade

Built by developer Benjamin Fink at the height of the Melbourne Land Boom, the Block Arcade became a popular haunt for Melbourne's social elite. With 30 shops, it was the grandest and most opulent of the many retail arcades which were developed throughout the city at the time. The Block Arcade was built on an L shaped plan with a glazed polygonal atrium space at the elbow.

280-286 Collins Street and 96-102 Elizabeth Street, Melbourne   *Architect - Twentyman & Askew*

1891 *'Labassa', North Caulfield*

Canadian-born Alexander W Robertson instructed JAB Koch to design the "most magnificent house in Melbourne" and was rewarded with the overblown exuberance of 'Ontario' (renamed 'Labassa' in 1896). An Italianate interpretation of the German Renaissance, the interiors of 'Labassa' feature a layering of heavily gilded and embossed wallpapers, gilded and stenciled ceilings, stained glass, and parquet floors.

2 Manor Grove, North Caulfield   *Architect - JAB Koch*

Spotswood Pumping Station   1893-96

The Spotswood Pumping Station, designed in a French Classical Revival style, was a key component of Melbourne's first centralized sewerage system. Designed by E Kussman, the Pumping Station housed ten large steam pumping engines by 1914, which were powered by coal-fired boilers. The works were fully electric by 1925, and were decommissioned in 1965. The Pumping Station is now part of the Scienceworks complex.

Douglas Parade, Spotswood

1897 *Springthorpe Memorial, Booroondara Cemetery*

As testament to both John Springthorpe's love of his wife Annie and his belief in the Arts and Crafts movement, Harold Desbrowe-Annear conceived of a sombre Greek Doric temple form with black granite columns and a grey granite entablature on a square plan. A flame-coloured leadlight domed ceiling illuminates a marble sculpture by Bertram McKennal of an angel of mercy attending to Annie Springthorpe.

Booroondara Cemetery, Park Hill Road, Kew   *Architect - Harold Desbrowe-Annear*

Cupples House, Camberwell 1900

The Cupples House is a classic example of the Domestic Queen Anne style so prominent at the turn of the century. The planning is typical of a house of this style, rotating off the central hall with gabled wings on an L shape beneath an all-embracing hipped roof. The exterior, notably devoid of symmetry, features terracotta tiles, turned timber verandah posts, red-brick walls, and ornamental gargoyles and finials.

608 Riversdale Road, Camberwell   *Architect - Ussher & Kemp*

1902

Milton House

Though attributed to Sydney Smith & Ogg, it is likely that their 'design consultant' Robert Haddon was mainly responsible for this design. The whimsical decoration of a Georgian style red-brick facade features many typical Haddon Art Nouveau details including curvilinear foliage ornamentation and a terracotta floral frieze.

21-25 Flinders Lane, Melbourne

Architect - Sydney Smith & Ogg

Chadwick House, Eaglemont 1903

The Chadwick House was built for Annear's father-in-law as one of three houses he designed on a sloping site. Incorporating a balloon frame, the exterior is painted brown and ochre, with spectacle-shaped verandahs framing the view to the Dandenongs. With its innovative open-planning, the dark stained-timber interior has many ingenious details including doors and windows which slide back into the wall cavities.

32-34 The Eyrie, Eaglemont

Architect - Harold Desbrowe-Annear.
Restoration by Peter Crone 1990-

1904 *Melbourne City Baths*

Working on a triangular site, the architects composed a grand Edwardian Baroque pile at the northern end of Swanston Street. The men's and the women's swimming pools have separate entrances on either side of the symmetrical approach from the street. The highly mannered classical composition of the façade is defined by the heavy symmetry, and a 'blood-and-bandage' red-brick and cream-render striping.

Swanston Street, Melbourne   *Architect - JJ & EJ Clark*

'Dalswraith', Kew **1906**

One of Henry Kemp's most accomplished designs, 'Dalswraith' (now Campion College) was an Old English reading of the Domestic Queen Anne style. The mansion was distinguished by its dominant walls and the sweeping approach of its driveway, rather than the then prevalent picturesque roofline and return verandah. Internally, the elaborate interior has a distinctly mediaeval ambience with Jacobean-inspired ceiling designs.

99 Studley Park Road, Kew   *Architect - Ussher & Kemp*

1911 *Bendigo Hotel, Collingwood*

The Bendigo Hotel was one of a number of hotels that Sydney Smith & Ogg designed for the Carlton Brewing Company. The design, a sinuous interpretation of the English Freestyle, or Art Nouveau, may be partially attributed to Robert Haddon, who was 'design consultant' to the firm, and incorporates many features typical of his work. The symmetrical massing of the hotel's forms is emphasized by the bulging oriel corner towers.

125 Johnston Street, Collingwood   *Architect - Sydney Smith & Ogg*

Flinders Street Station 1901-11

An enduring Melbourne landmark, Flinders Street Station is a massive Edwardian Baroque composition that symbolizes the pomp and majesty of the British Empire, bearing comparison with Indian colonial monuments of the time. The building presents a long red brick façade to Flinders Street, emphasized by cream-render 'bandages' and a punctuating clocktower which also terminates the Queen Street axis from the north.

Flinders Street, Melbourne   *Architect - JW Fawcett & HPC Ashworth (Railways Department)*

1913-15 *Barwon River Aqueduct, Geelong*

The Barwon River Ovoid Sewer Aqueduct crosses the Barwon floodplain 2 kilometres south of Geelong. It was designed by a firm who mainly built marine structures, including reinforced concrete ships and pontoons. The form of the 756 metres long, 14 span aqueduct was derived from the Firth of Forth rail bridge in Scotland (1889). The Barwon River Aqueduct was decommissioned in 1993.

Leather Street, Breakwater, Geelong   *Architect - Edward Giles Stone and Ernest J Siddley*

Missions to Seamen 1917

The Missions to Seamen building is an intriguing Spanish-influenced rendition of an Arts and Crafts building, and is one of the earliest Spanish-influenced buildings in Melbourne. The design is distinguished by the hemispherical stupa-like form of the gymnasium, which owes much of its inspiration to WR Lethaby, Butler's English mentor. Originally to be constructed in red brick, the building is rendered with rough-cast concrete.

717 Flinders Street, Melbourne   *Architect - Walter R Butler*

1917 *Lippincott House, Eaglemont*

A Prairie-style rendition of an Arts and Crafts house, exhibiting Japanese influences in its roof profile, situated on the Griffin-planned Glenard Estate, adjacent to Griffin's own diminutive house, 'Pholiota' (1920). The estate demonstrated many of Griffin's suburban planning ideals, the most important being a shared landscape defined by Australian native plants.

21 Glenard Drive, Eaglemont   *Architect - Roy Lippincott and Walter Burley Griffin*

Newman College, University of Melbourne 1915-18

The Catholic Church's residential college at Melbourne University is one of the Griffins' most intriguing designs. Only half of the intended building was completed, a long low cloister on an L plan defined at its junction by a rotunda which housed the dining room. The massive structure of reinforced concrete faced with sandstone reveals a romantic mixture of influences with an overriding mediaeval ambience.

University of Melbourne, Swanston Street, Parkville

Architect - Walter Burley Griffin
and Marion Mahony

1920 *'Pebbles', Footscray*

A well-preserved example of the Californian bungalow house type which became so prevalent in the 1920s. The distinguishing elements of the bungalow were spreading gabled roofs, rough rendering, Marseilles tiles, and robust timberwork. Pebbles are a continuing decorative theme through this house, with external piers coated in crushed quartz, and water-washed pebbles adorn the fireplace surround.

57A Droop Street, Footscray   *Architect - Schreiber & Jörgensen*

Dendy Street Bathing Boxes, Brighton   1920s

The Dendy Street bathing boxes are typical of the many endearing colourful structures which once lined Melbourne's bayside beaches, including Mordialloc, Mornington, Mentone, Aspendale and Mount Martha. Nearly 80 boxes remain near Dendy Street, a reminder of the wheeled bathing boxes which were available at Brighton from the 1840s. Permanent bathing boxes were erected from the mid-1870s.

Dendy Street, Brighton

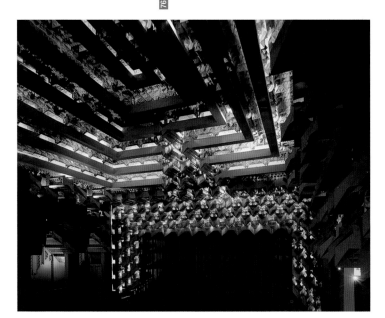

1921-24 *Capitol Theatre*

The Griffins' Capitol Theatre is an Aladdin's Cave of exotic forms and dramatic illumination. The plaster ceiling was renowned for its spectacular lightshow as hidden coloured lights were gradually revealed to the audience. Reinforced concrete portals enable the suspension of the ceiling above a column free interior. The original lobby and vestibules were replaced by a shopping arcade in the 1960s, but the cinema and its ceiling remain.

109-117 Swanston Street, Melbourne

Architect - Walter Burley Griffin and Marion Mahony
with Peck & Kempter

Church Street Bridge, Richmond 1920-24

Graceful Edwardian Baroque stylings decorate a bridge consisting of three reinforced concrete arches with arcaded infills. The paired lighting pylons define the roadway, and lend a formal processional quality which clearly articulates Annear's 'City Beautiful' beliefs. The bridge's engineer was JA Laing, and it was built by John Monash's Re-inforced Concrete and Monier Pipe Constructing Company.

Church Street, Richmond   *Architect - Harold Desbrowe-Annear and TR Ashworth*

1928

Forum Theatre

The exotic design of the Forum Theatre (formerly the State Theatre and the Rapallo Cinema) has many stylistic influences. The Moorish layering of the exterior is matched internally by the Mediterranean sky ceiling with a moon and stars, a balcony 'borrowed' from the Doge's Palace in Venice, a Florentine Garden, and a pergola adorned with artificial vines which runs the length of the dress circle.

150 Flinders Street, Melbourne

Architect - Bohringer Taylor & Johnson

1929

Majorca House

The Spanish/Moorish façade of Majorca House is faced in blue terracotta faience with gold ornamental details. The building terminates Degraves Street and can be seen dramatically rising up on its site from Flinders Street. The design was informed by Norris's appreciation of Spanish Colonial Revival architecture, which was gained from a visit to California in the 1920s.

Architect - Harry Norris

1929-32

Manchester Unity Building

The Commercial Modern Gothic form of the Manchester Unity Building was directly inspired by Raymond Hood's design for the Chicago Tribune Tower of 1922. Faced in gold-brown glazed faience and decorated with figures of benevolence and charity, the Manchester Unity Building forms the prow of a notable streetscape created by the 132-foot height restriction (applied to city buildings in 1916).

91 Swanston Street, Melbourne   *Architect - Marcus Barlow*

Shrine of Remembrance 1927-34

The design of the Shrine of Remembrance resulted from a world-wide competition, won by Victorian returned soldiers, Philip Hudson and James Wardrop. Their entry was influenced by details from classical Greek monuments, with the cubic form and stepped pyramid roof derived from the Mausoleum of Halicarnassus (353 BC). The World War 2 Memorial Forecourt (1950-54) was designed by Ernest Milston.

St Kilda Road and Birdwood Avenue, Melbourne   *Architect - Hudson & Wardrop*

1934

MacRobertson Girls High School

This school was the first significant local interpretation of the cream-brick architecture of Dutch modernist Willem Dudok, as exemplified at Hilversum Town Hall (1927-31). The School was financed by a donation to the State Government from Sir MacPherson Robertson to mark Melbourne's Centenary. The flat-roofed design was highlighted with vermillion steel-framed windows and glazed blue sill bricks, with a signature Moderne flagpole.

Albert Road and Kings Way, South Melbourne

Architect - Seabrook and Fildes

Former McPherson's Building **1934-37**

The McPherson's Building is Melbourne's most successful interpretation of horizontality in architecture. Designed in the Streamlined Moderne style as a warehouse, office and showroom for Sir William McPherson's hardware company, the building is composed of three dominant horizontal spandrels separating the sheer expanses of glass. The western stair tower provides an emphatic termination to the horizontal banding.

546-566 Collins Street, Melbourne   *Architect - Reid & Pearson in association with Stuart P. Calder*

1937 *Heidelberg Municipal Offices and Town Hall*

The Heidelberg Town Hall is a massive and formally designed interpretation of Willem Dudok's Hilversum Town Hall (1927-31). The tower owes its form directly to this building, centering a picturesque hybrid of Modern and Moderne design in cream-brick, with an abstracted temple front and flanking pavilions.

253-277 Upper Heidelberg Road, Ivanhoe

Architect - Peck & Kempter in association with AC Leith & Associates

1940-43

Former Russell Street Police Headquarters

This Beaux Arts skyscraper was designed by Percy Everett, Chief Architect of the Public Works Department from 1934 to 1953. The stepped tower and steel-framed communications tower give the Police Headquarters a Gotham City profile, which was utilized in many television drama programmes, most notably 'Homicide'.

354 Russell Street, Melbourne   *Architect – Percy Everett (Public Works Department)*

1945-50 *'Stanhill'*

The largest in a series of flats which were designed by Swiss émigré Frederick Romberg before he commenced his partnership with Roy Grounds and Robin Boyd in 1953. The reinforced concrete flats are an amalgamation of International Modern motifs and the stylistic influences of Alvar Aalto and Le Corbusier, among others. Each of the building's elevations reveals a different composition of details and sculptural massing.

34 Queens Road, Melbourne   *Architect - Frederick Romberg*

Grounds House, Toorak 1954

A result of Roy Grounds' experiments with creating architectural forms from pure geometry, the Grounds House was the forerunner to the National Gallery of Victoria (1959-68). The square plan with a circular internal courtyard creates a house which is completely inward looking, as the external facade is only punctuated by a high line of windows. An oversized front door features a Grounds signature doorknocker.

24 Hill Street, Toorak   *Architect - Roy Grounds*

1955 *McIntyre House, Kew*

The McIntyre House was built on a steep wooded slope above the Yarra River. Contained in one precariously cantilevered elongated triangle suspended from another A-frame triangle, the house presents a dramatic sight when viewed from the Yarra and the Victoria Street Bridge. The house was originally painted with bright primary colours, and was the first of what is now a riverbank compound for the McIntyre family.

2 Hodgson Street, Kew   *Architect - Peter and Dione McIntyre*

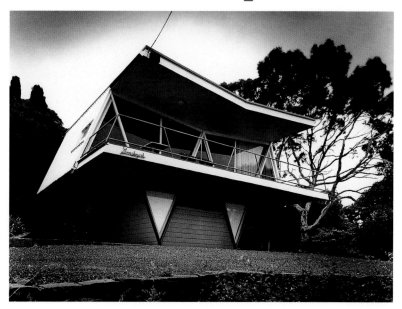

McCraith House, Dromana 1956

The McCraith House was built as a small holiday house on the steep hillside beneath Arthurs Seat. Designed by David Chancellor and Rex Patrick, the expressive structure comprises four triangular frames resting on just four points, topped by an inverted butterfly roof. The almost cartoon-like visage of the house, which could be likened to a pair of binoculars or sunglasses, gazes across Port Philip Bay to the city in the distance.

Atunga Terrace and Caldwell Road, Dromana   *Architect - Chancellor & Patrick*

1952-56 *Wilson Hall, University of Melbourne*

This beautifully crafted box-building replaced the original Wilson Hall (1879), designed by Joseph Reed in the Gothic Revival style, which had burned down in 1952. Designed by Osborn McCutcheon, each of the four external façades has an individual expression, and the finely veneered Swedish birch interior features a huge biomorphic mural by Douglas Annand. The furniture for the dais was designed by Grant Featherston.

Wilson Avenue, University of Melbourne, Parkville   *Architect - Bates Smart & McCutcheon*

1955-58
ICI House

ICI (now Orica) House was the first building to break Melbourne's 132-foot height limit (set in 1916), as the plan provided for open space at ground level. This took the form of a garden designed by landscape architect John Stevens with a sculpted fountain by Gerald Lewers. The building itself is an especially elegant and refined prismatic slab sheathed in a blue glass curtain wall.

1 Nicholson Street, East Melbourne

Architect - Bates Smart & McCutcheon

1959 *Sidney Myer Music Bowl*

A feat of engineering as much as architecture, the design of the Myer Music Bowl by Barry Patten was developed in partnership with structural engineers WL Irwin & Associates. The structure was based on a complex web of pre-stressed steel cables supporting a taut skin of aluminum-faced plywood panels, above two tapering cigar-shaped masts. The Bowl has been extensively renovated and restored by Gregory Burgess (2001).

Kings Domain, Melbourne

Architect - Yuncken Freeman Brothers,
Griffiths & Simpson (Barry Patten – Design Architect)

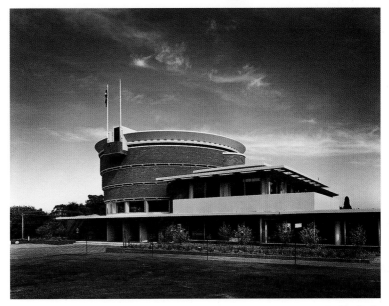

Brighton Municipal Offices 1960

The former Brighton Municipal Offices, now the local library, are a tribute to Frank Lloyd Wright's Guggenheim Museum, New York (1946-59). Sitting atop a flat slab of offices and facilities, the tapering red-brick drum contains a ceramic mural and spiral ramp within the circular public lobby, with peacock blue furnishings by Grant Featherston.

15 Boxshall Street, Brighton   *Architect - Oakley & Parkes (Kevin Knight – Design Architect)*

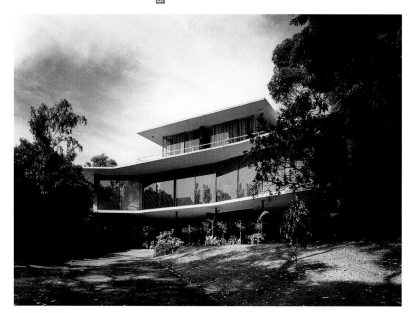

1961 *Delbridge House, Eaglemont*

A classic 1960s home, the Delbridge house was designed by its non-architect owners with structural engineering advice from RMIT lecturer Emery Balint. A floating minimalist exterior of glass and unbelievably thin reinforced concrete floor slabs conceals a 'featurist' interior, which incorporates Castlemaine stone walls with cantilevered stairs and balustrades of overlapping brass squares.

55 Carlsberg Road, Eaglemont   *Designed and built by the owner*

Jimmy Watson's Wine Bar, Carlton 1962

Robin Boyd designed Jimmy Watson's Wine Bar whilst in partnership with Frederick Romberg. The construction saw the merging of three separate 19th century terrace shops and residences, evidenced by the remaining internal brick party walls. The white-painted façade evokes a Mediterranean presence appropriate to the Italian heritage and streetscape of Lygon Street.

333 Lygon Street, Carlton   *Architect - Romberg & Boyd*

1965

Museum of Modern Art at Heide

Heide II, now the Museum of Modern Art at Heide, was designed by David McGlashan as a house for John and Sunday Reed, and was memorably defined by Neil Clerehan as "International style set down amongst the melaleucas". The interlocking sequence of L shaped walls built from Mt Gambier limestone have created a maze surrounding the house itself, which contains a wonderful double height gallery space. A 15 acre sculpture garden slopes down to the Yarra.

7 Templestowe Road, Bulleen   *Architect - McGlashan & Everist*

St Thomas's Church, Langwarrin 1966

St Thomas's Anglican Church was funded by the bequest of the novelist Neville Shute. The jagged organic concrete buttresses are covered with an aggregate of Dromana granite and Cave Hill limestone. The sharp forms are emphasized by the severely pointed gables and the zig-zag pattern of the stained-glass panels. The internal joinery and finishes are of mountain ash and Queensland maple, and the doors are sheathed in copper.

Corner North Road and Warrandyte Road, Langwarrin   *Architect - Wystan, Widdows and David Caldwell*

1966 *Fooks House, North Caulfield*

Czechoslovakian architect Ernest Fooks migrated to Australia from Austria, via Canada, in 1939.
His own house has a street façade of heavily textured, informally shaped brick screen walls. Internal
courtyards, patios, and freestanding walls create a continuum between house and garden. The sinuous
flow of the vaulted ceiling in the living room is emphasized by multiple thin strips of mountain ash.

32 Howitt Road, North Caulfield   *Architect - Ernest Fooks*

1959-68

National Gallery of Victoria

An elaboration of Grounds' earlier design for his own home (1954), the National Gallery of Victoria is a monumental bluestone building inspired by Italian palazzi and the Old Melbourne Gaol, with an Oriental ambience. Rectangular in plan, the three square enclosed courtyards emphasize the internal focus. Notable features of the Gallery include the Richardsonian entry arch, the waterwall, and the Leonard French stained-glass ceiling in the Great Hall.

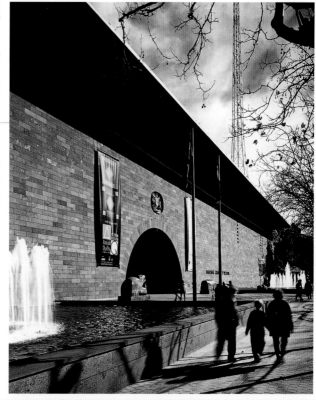

St Kilda Road, Melbourne

Architect - Roy Grounds

1969

Featherston House, Ivanhoe

Grant and Mary Featherston had declared "We wish we could live in a courtyard", and Robin Boyd's ensuing design enclosed an exposed garden of moss and ivy between parallel brick walls, a unique live-in glasshouse with fully glazed walls at either end. Solid timber platforms beneath a translucent roof float down the slope to Darebin Creek, the only vertical element in the home being the massive brick fireplace.

22 The Boulevard, Ivanhoe   *Architect - Romberg & Boyd*

1967-72

BHP House

Not surprisingly, BHP House was intended to promote the use of steel in building construction. The severe Chicago styling of the building openly borrowed from the work of the American firm Skidmore Owings & Merrill, indeed seeking their advice for the engineering of the building. The tower incorporates a central steel-framed core, a steel and glass façade, steel trusses linking the core and the façade, and a steel deck flooring system.

140 William Street, Melbourne

Architect - Yuncken Freeman

1983

No. 1 Collins Street

The construction of No. 1 Collins Street was unusual for the time as it involved the restoration of several historic buildings on the site. The new tower steps back respectfully from the street, allowing the original buildings to retain their identity, while establishing a deftly modeled and contextually appropriate gateway to the city.

1 Collins Street, Melbourne   *Architect - Denton Corker Marshall in association with Robert Peck YFHK*

Grant / Collins House, Officer **1986**

A consolidation of many of the themes that Guilford Bell had been exploring throughout his career, the Grant / Collins house is his expression of a country villa. Bell referred to the white corrugated iron house as being "like a handkerchief dropped on the site". The formal landscaping, featuring a parterre garden and a large dammed lily pond, complements the symmetrical planning of the house.

Whiteside Road, Officer   *Architect - Guilford Bell*

1984

Macrae and Way Studios, South Melbourne

The Macrae and Way Film Production Office is a whimsical and irreverent surviving design from the short-lived Biltmoderne, an architectural practice comprising Dale Jones-Evans, Roger Wood and Randal Marsh. The work is typically exuberant, a pointy-eared wall facing the small cobbled street is adorned with a large mirrored cartouche and covered with concrete rosettes, studding the face of an architectural cartoon character.

3 Francis Street, South Melbourne   *Architect - Biltmoderne*

1990

Box Hill Community Arts Centre

Departing from the stark designs of his contemporaries, Gregory Burgess created a resolutely Arts and Crafts-inspired collaboration with Box Hill's community artists and ceramists, and the landscape architects Kate Cullity and Kevin Taylor. The rippling anthropomorphic forms of the Centre, appearing as if an eruption from the earth, are covered with pink, orange, and blue glazed bricks and tiles.

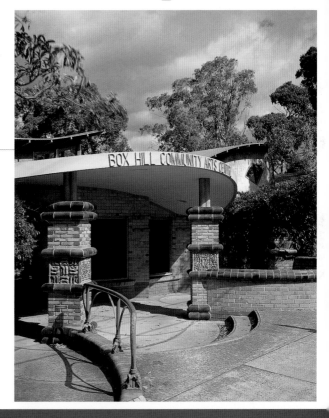

470 Station Street, Box Hill   *Architect - Gregory Burgess*

1990
101 Collins Street
(right of picture)

A Melbourne interpretation of a New York skyscraper, with a façade which steps back repeatedly to terminate in a pinnacle. The building's entry lobby was completed by the New York firm of Johnson and Burgee.

1991
120 Collins Street
(left of picture)

120 Collins Street also references New York skyscrapers, specifically reflecting the Art Deco profiles of the 1920s and 1930s. The graphic articulation of the façade reinforces the penetration of the slender tower into the city skyline.

101 Collins Street, Melbourne
Architect - Denton Corker Marshall

120 Collins Street, Melbourne
Architect - Daryl Jackson in association with Hassell Architects

Great Southern Stand, MCG **1992**

The Great Southern Stand precinct, accommodating 60,000 spectators, was a controversial replacement of the original Southern Stand, built in 1937. It is a dramatic and expressive addition to the MCG's historic sequence of stands, with a thorny roofline of steel masts, trusses and supports. The movement of spectators through the building is graphically articulated with inclined ramps punctured by porthole windows.

Melbourne Cricket Ground, Brunton Avenue, Jolimont   *Architect - Daryl Jackson in association with Tompkins Shaw & Evans*

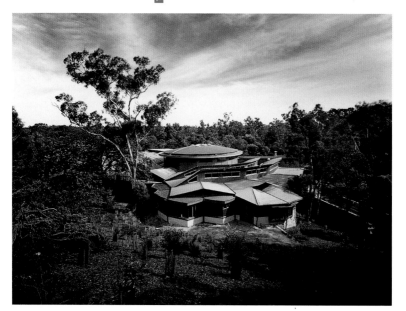

1994 *Eltham Library*

An organically massed building with a flower-like cross–section and a panoptic plan, the Library has a restless presence in the Eltham bushland. The mudbrick exterior on a brick base, raised above ground to prevent any potential flooding, is surrounded by broad eaves and verandahs. The interior, with ceiling battens of Victorian mountain ash, is lit by a layering of clerestorey windows.

Panther Place, Eltham   *Architect - Gregory Burgess*

Melbourne Terrace Apartments 1994

Nonda Katsalidis designed numerous highly-sculpted urban apartment blocks in the 1990s, distinguished by an intense interest in materials, their textures, and their capacity to weather. The Melbourne Terraces, are a complex layering of copper oxide-etched balconies, weathered metal, mannered window surrounds, glass blocks, and off-form concrete. Figurative sculptures by Peter Corlett mark the four entrances.

Corner Franklin and Queen Streets, Melbourne   *Architect - Katsalidis Architects*

1991-94

RMIT Building 8

Building 8 was the first of series of landmark buildings commissioned by RMIT University in the 1990s, and is an extremely colourful pronouncement of the University's presence on Swanston Street. Edmond & Corrigan's design incorporates a 1977 building by John Andrews. The elaborately detailed façade and expressionist roofscape utilize an eclectic architectural vocabulary, presenting individualistic elevations to both Swanston Street and Bowen Street to the rear.

Swanston Street, Melbourne

Architect - Edmond & Corrigan with Demaine Partnership

1992-95

Storey Hall, RMIT

The fluorescent green and purple façade of Storey Hall is festooned with a complex pattern of interlocking diamond-shaped panels, and the interior lobby spaces are shaped by folded walls and ceilings. The façade of the adjoining Hibernian Hall has been retained, and its auditorium transformed by an otherworldly ceiling, referencing the pentagonal geometries of Roger Penrose. The crumpled metal panels of the new façade are inscribed with the words 'Resurrection City'.

344-346 Swanston Street, Melbourne

Architect - Ashton Raggatt McDougall
(Hibernian Hall, 1887, by Tappin Gilbert & Dennehy)

1995

Promedicus, Burnley

ARM's concept for the Promedicus Medical Centre transformed an existing 19th century State Bank building. With an inversion of negative and positive space, the glazed west wall was formed by the impression of an invisible Buckminster Fuller geodesic dome, a nod to the application of technology required by a medical computing firm. The process was described by the architects as "taking a bite out of the building".

450 Swan Street, Burnley

Architect - Ashton Raggatt McDougall

Melbourne Exhibition Centre **1996**

The elegant linear elevation and roof-lines of the Melbourne Exhibition Centre address the Yarra River with a DCM signature angled blade saluting the city. An external colonnade with a forest of angled 'stick' columns adjoins a glazed public concourse. The lobby spaces contain an array of colourful shapes and forms, disguising the concrete remains of an abandoned scheme to build a new Museum of Victoria in the 1980s.

Clarendon Street, South Melbourne   *Architect - Denton Corker Marshall*

1996

Silo Apartments, Richmond

The dynamic prow-like profile of the Silo Apartments is created by the addition of a northern tower to four existing Daly's Malthouse wheat silos. The six-storey building contains one apartment per floor, with a bedroom in each of three silos, while the fourth contains a stair and bathroom. The living-rooms are in the northern addition. The rusted steel of the balconies and the perforated crowning eaves combine with off-form concrete to establish a rugged urban presence.

22 Abinger Street. Richmond

Architect - Katsalidis Architects

Godsell House, Kew 1997

Sean Godsell's own house is veiled with weathered steel gridded screens, and cantilevers 5.5 metres out from its site towards the street. The rectangular plan is divided internally by a single wall, with the spaces opened up or closed down by sliding screens. The low-lying native garden of grass tussocks and large boulders was designed by Gordon Ford, and is the perfect foil to the rusted house-as-cage.

6 Hodgson Street, Kew   *Architect - Sean Godsell*

1998

Building 220, RMIT Bundoora

This building is a bold experiment in colour and texture on a nondescript outlying university campus. A curving bright orange 'bridge' clad with metal panels runs between grey rusticated concrete abutments which are randomly perforated with porthole windows. Wood Marsh (with PINK) were the designers for an equally sculptural set of buildings at Deakin University's Burwood campus in 1996.

RMIT Bundoora Campus, Plenty Road, Bundoora

Architect - Wood Marsh with
Pels Innes Neilson & Kosloff (PINK)

1999

Bourke Street Footbridge and Gateway

Two plum-coloured pylons marked by flashing bands of red neon create a dramatic termination to Bourke Street, acting as signposts to the footbridge leading to the Dockland precinct and Colonial Stadium. Ramps cut through the pylons, and quizzical red steel 'antlers' ending in fluorescent light tubes line the footbridge. The project is a colourful realization of Wood Marsh's vision of urban design as public art.

Bourke Street and Spencer Street, Melbourne

Architect – Wood Marsh

1999

Melbourne City Link Gateway

Denton Corker Marshall saw their design for the envisaged international gateway to Melbourne as a "modern urban architectural sculpture". This sculpture incorporates a monumental yellow beam cantilevering 70 metres over the freeway, 39 red-painted angled columns 30 metres high, an orange undulating sound-barrier wall, and a snaking 300 metre elliptical metal 'sound tube'.

City Link Tollway near Flemington Road exit

Architect - Denton Corker Marshall

2000

Republic Tower

With the sculptural profile of an armour-clad samurai warrior, the Republic Tower apartments are built from off-form concrete, stainless steel and glass. A huge combination of a concave and a convex billboard addresses the street corner as the site for a constantly changing display of public art, commissioned by the Visible Art Foundation. Shops, a café, and a restaurant are incorporated behind a timber pergola which faces La Trobe Street.

Corner Queen Street and La Trobe Street, Melbourne

Architect - Katsalidis Architects

2000 *Melbourne Museum*

The dramatic architectural gestures of the Melbourne Museum are a manifestation of the institution's need to reinvent its image for the 21st Century. The various galleries and components of the Museum are individually articulated, and accessed from a central promenade. All are contained beneath a formal gridded volumetric framework. Three soaring roof blades proclaim the Museum's public presence to the city.

Rathdowne Street, Carlton   *Architect - Denton Corker Marshall*

Wardle House, Kew 2000

John Wardle's own home, both a continuation and a summary of his preceding body of residential work, is an addition to a 1951 house by Horace Tribe. Detailed with black plate steel and textured timber cladding, the house is angled into the site around existing elm trees. The picture window facing the street reveals an intricately crafted interior. With this house, John Wardle has created the beautiful out of the everyday.

Kevin Grove, Kew   *Architect - John Wardle*

2001 *Drum House, Fitzroy*

Kerstin Thompson's insertion of a monumental glazed drum within the body of a former sheet metal factory is an ingenious rethink on the potential of inner-suburban warehouse conversion. There has been no attempt to have the space masquerade as a typical house, as it resists the usual approach of adapting a smart interior fitout to an existing shell. The drum is both an outdoor space and a daylight lantern for the surrounding living areas.

Architect - Kerstin Thompson

VUT On-Line Training Centre, St Albans **2001**

Lyons' ongoing preoccupation with a building's 'skin' has enlivened many mundane suburban landscapes. The architects (three brothers – Corbett, Cameron, and Carey Lyon) faced this building with 'Vitrapanel' cladding, decorated with an abstract melting brown and yellow pattern. The psychedelic façade forms a visual pronouncement of the brothers' ideologies, or as they would have it – "EYE-deology".

Victoria University of Technology, McKechnie Street, St Albans   *Architect - Lyons Architects*

INDEX